The
Anatomy
of Riding

The Anatomy of Riding

Sara Wyche

The Crowood Press

First published in 2004 by
The Crowood Press Ltd
Ramsbury, Marlborough
Wiltshire SN8 2HR

www.crowood.com

British Library Cataloguing in Publication Data
A catalogue record for this book is available from the British Library.

ISBN 1 86126 624 3

Dedication
To Elizabeth, whose book this is; and to Jim, for his encouragement while it was being created.

Acknowledgements
The author would like to thank Hannah Brown, George Rex and *Horse & Rider* magazine for
their help with the cover.

Cover: Hannah Brown on George Rex

Line-drawings by Sara Wyche

Edited and designed by OutHouse Publishing Services,
Shalbourne, Marlborough, Wiltshire SN8 3QJ

Printed and bound in Great Britain by CPI, Bath

Contents

Author's Note

The reader may be surprised to see that many of the riders depicted in the diagrams are drawn without clothes. There are two reasons for this. The first is that clothing fashions come and go, and some types of clothing have become associated with particular branches of the sport. The second is that, underneath our boots and jods, we are all human beings. Our clothes (boots, chaps, gloves, back-protectors, and so on) have a certain impact on the way we ride, but in the end riding is just the act of the human sitting on the horse; fundamentally, clothes don't change this.

Every effort has been made to draw the horse's anatomy as accurately as possible. The muscles are shown with their correct places of origin and insertion. However, in order to avoid burying the real subject of this book – the art of riding – under a mountain of anatomical jargon, terminology has been simplified unless the scientific names are necessary to differentiate between related structures. Any reader who wants a complete overview of the muscles is referred to *The Horse's Muscles in Motion* (also published by The Crowood Press).

Finally, many of the anatomical diagrams show the horse's joints in the form of mechanical shapes. These shapes are approximations. For example, if the main axis of movement is backwards and forwards, like a barrel hinge, then the joint has been drawn as a hinge. If the joint swivels like a ball-and-socket then it has been drawn as such.

Whilst one might quibble about the one per cent of joint movement that falls outside these parameters, this form of representation is by and large accurate enough. It has been chosen to help the rider see, at a single glance, the true movement possibilities of the horse. In the words of the philosopher, Krishnamurti:

It is one of the most difficult things to convey something, which not only demands the accurate use of words, but also an accuracy of perception that lies beyond these words ... a sense of intimate contact with reality.
The Impossible Question (new ed., 2003, Orion)

Preface

What is it that enables us to ride the horse? What makes it possible for us to take charge of the horse's body and cause it to jump an obstacle taller than the horse himself, or to trace an intricate pattern of steps across the empty space of an arena? How can we usurp this extraordinary resource in muscular power and agility? What puts us in control? Ultimately it is the horse's natural disposition to trust, to be obedient, and to respond consistently to a given set of stimuli. In addition, he does so not just with his head, or with his heart, but with his entire body. His willingness makes him exceptionally trainable; his submissiveness may make him vulnerable.

Because the horse is acutely perceptive, there is almost no end to the range of stimuli we can use to produce – from the human point of view – a desired response. The cues can be visual, tactile, or acoustic. They can consist of tension and release, reward and reprimand. In fact, they can be anything that derives from the human language of coercion. Any cue may become absorbed into the language of riding horses.

But how do you begin to teach such a language, one that in an instant can change from the sharp point of a spur to the subtle innuendo of a half-halt? It virtually requires every pupil and teacher to share one body and mind in order to gain that necessary rider 'feel'. Teaching someone to ride a horse is the most difficult task because there are no common base lines. When you teach someone to drive a car, you teach the skills to control a machine that has no imagination. When you teach someone to play a musical instrument, you teach them to bring to life an object that is otherwise inanimate. However, when you teach someone to ride, there are always two sets of variables: two bodies and two distinctly independent minds.

In traditional riding lessons the most usual way of communicating with the pupil is via the spoken word (in other words, yelling across the arena). Yet riding is a skill that requires a high degree of precision, and verbal language is the most imprecise means of communication imaginable: it is always open to interpretation. Words like 'elastic' or 'tense' can occupy very different spheres in an individual's understanding. Even 'left' and 'right' is a challenge to some. Meanwhile, the horse bravely follows the cues, using movements he thinks are most appropriate, even if his ultimate reward is to spend half an hour trotting remorselessly round on his forehand.

Instead of teaching people 'how to ride' – how to 'do' shoulder-in, to 'do' walk to canter transitions, half-pass, and so on – perhaps we should teach people how it is possible to ride: how it is possible to take a single coherent system of body language and make the horse's anatomy work for us – in any situation and without causing harm to the horse.

This book, in words and diagrams, is an attempt to describe how to implement such a system. There is nothing new: the techniques have been described by great horsemen, past and present. However, by using simple line-drawings this book illustrates why some riding techniques are anatomically logical for the horse while others are anatomically flawed. It describes what really goes on beneath the saddle, regardless of traditionally held views or modern – sometimes quirky – opinion.

There are many good books on riding, some factual, some thought-provoking, some inspirational. This book is not designed to compete with any of them. Instead, it is meant to be used alongside them, to illuminate and underpin them. Used in this way, it can help you to become your own teacher and to journey inside the anatomy of riding.

Introduction

The art of riding is a celebration of motion, of nature's rhythms.

> Paul Belasik, *Exploring Dressage Technique*, 1994

The art of riding embraces a great many disciplines, many of which make specialist use of particular aspects of the horse's movements. This book is unashamedly biased towards dressage, not just because it is the author's passion but because it is – or should be – the foundation of all other riding activities. Call it dressage, or call it simply flatwork, the ability to have accurate command over the horse's paces is the building block upon which all other forms of equestrian sport rest. Without it, the rider may ride with skill, but he doesn't necessarily ride with understanding.

We live in the age of analysis. Other centuries have been characterized by their 'enlightenment', 'classicism', or 'romanticism', but we live in an age that is driven by the need to analyse and inform – to the extent that not only do we sometimes not see the wood for the trees but we are often in danger of getting caught up in the twigs. This applies to trends in horsemanship just as much as it does to any other aspect of modern life.

The analysis of horsemanship, and advice on the principles of riding, is not new. The Greek Xenophon gave us what is probably the earliest, most complete written treatise. But long before Xenophon wrote *The Art of Horsemanship* (in the 4th century BC), riding skills were documented and illustrated, not in so many words, perhaps, but in pictorial decorations on pottery, buildings or, in the beginning, on walls in caves.

What *is* new is that advice on riding techniques no longer serves the ultimate purpose of improving the cavalry rider for the good of his country. Instead, it has become the stock-in-trade of monthly magazines and journals, which encapsulate popular riding culture and provide a shop window for today's riders and trainers, who now come from a wide variety of equestrian disciplines.

Using the medium of the press, top riders – from different backgrounds and with vastly differing opinions – can showcase their methods of training before a huge cross-section of the riding public. This has led to a wealth of interest in the different ways of riding horses. For many people this information has become an important source of inspiration and support. But there is another dimension.

The printed word is extremely potent, and even more so when the content is reinforced by bold photographs and diagrams. Articles in magazines might seem, at face value, to be casual entertainment. Nevertheless, we should take them quite seriously. They are, after all a form of analysis. Analysis is fine, as long as it discusses facts and is without sentiment. Done properly it should promote awareness. But it is also capable of creating divisions. And that is a problem when deciding how best to ride the horse.

For example, what does it mean to 'ride the horse correctly'? It could be argued that the willingness of successful riders to share their preferred methods of training means that horse owners can make an informed choice between different styles to suit themselves, their horses, their lifestyles, and their ambitions. In reality, such is the sheer volume of

9

information available – in books, magazines, on video, on tap – that advice on how to ride has become fragmented. It is confusing, and even contradictory. It is now virtually impossible to find a common thread, in other words a single, underlying principle that is the art of riding horses.

Some years ago, I listened to a dressage rider as she explained how her trainer had gone to great lengths to analyse the relative positions of the horse's seven neck vertebrae, not only during each of the paces but in the transitions between the paces. This seemed a rather intellectual and unnecessary exercise to me since it focused on a chain of biomechanical events that should not be the concern of the rider – if he is riding the horse correctly. If the rider has to interfere with the position of the horse's neck it is usually the result of negative control.

At about the time this lady was grappling with the movements of the horse's neck (some twenty years ago), dressage as a sport was up-and-coming in Britain. Today, dressage is hugely popular, and yet there are some riders that have rejected it, having witnessed methods of training that seemed forced, unnatural, and frankly unfair to the horse. If 'on the bit' could be achieved only by means of tortured expressions, artificially imposed gestures, and an exaggerated display of effort, they argued that this could not be a reasonable use of the horse's natural resources.

Those for whom the act of absolute submission in the horse is repellent have sought an alternative way, for example in Western riding and 'Natural Horse-Man-Ship' (*see* page 12). However, in their quest for a freer form of self-expression in riding they are not always blameless of replacing 'on the bit' with 'on the forehand'.

Whatever one's creed in riding – conventional or natural – most riders would probably agree that to ride the horse correctly means to ride him humanely, logically, and, if possible, in an aesthetically pleasing way. Yet, these qualities need a firm definition, a single common denom-inator, one based on incontrovertible evidence. Where do we look for such evidence? It's written in the structure of the horse's anatomy.

One evening, a client of mine was describing a riding lesson she had just had with a visiting trainer. During the lesson she had been told to balance her horse by turning his head outwards, towards the perimeter fence of the arena. It so happened that the horse in question was new and that, in the process of getting to know him, the rider had uncovered a number of physical problems: a sore back, a tilted pelvis, and a strained shoulder. She had originally come to me for veterinary advice, but after a programme of physiotherapy, chiropractic, acupuncture, modifications to the shoeing, and a much-needed overhaul of the saddle, she had also asked for advice on the horse's schooling.

The horse was a stocky cob, with a short neck, a long back, and a 'downhill' posture. He had a way of going that was typically 'right-handed': he pushed off predominantly with the right hind leg, which had caused the right gluteal muscles to become overbuilt, and – in order to keep his balance – tucked his left foreleg under his chest. This tipped him on to the outside edge of the left forefoot, putting a strain on the ligaments on the outside of the left fetlock, 'knee' and shoulder joints. The muscles at the base of the neck and on the left side of the chest were overdeveloped and tense from the effort of compensation.

During my own training in dressage, it had been instilled in me that the rider should, at all costs, avoid any excessive intervention of the outside rein that causes the horse to fall on to, and therefore overload, the inside shoulder – a maxim that is not always easy to follow given that dressage requires the horse to perform numerous changes of direction and bend.

My advice to this lady was to practise first establishing a contact with the outside rein and then taking up the inside rein to introduce the bend. When the horse offered to flex his neck in the direction of the bend, the rider should periodically relax the contact with the inside hand while maintaining the support with pressure from the inside leg. In this way, the horse would gradually come to realize that the left hand of *this* rider was never going to be an impenetrable barrier, and he could stop using his left foreleg like a crutch. However, in the most recent lesson, this rider had been given a completely different set of instructions: in fact they were the exact opposite of mine. As the conversation came to a close, she summarized by saying, 'Of course, *you* want the horse to be much more "up together" in front.' I was mortified.

The reason I was so upset had nothing to do with the merits of the inside versus the outside rein aids. Instead, it had everything to do with the fact that the client had missed the point – because I had failed to make it. I had not made it clear that my prescribed way of going for this horse was not just a matter of style or personal preference; it was a matter of protecting the horse's anatomy.

The anatomy of the horse (or biomechanics, which is the anatomy in movement) is the foundation for the art of riding. It is only by virtue of this unique physical structure that the horse can fulfil so many varied tasks. Yet it is remarkable that many people can ride for years without ever understanding how this anatomy works – because nobody tells them.

Imagine, for example, learning to drive a car by being allowed to crunch the gears until you just happen, by accident, to produce a smooth gear shift. Imagine learning to play a musical instrument by making all sorts of hideous noises until you hit on a means of producing a single pleasing note. Learning by trial and error is one way. But it is spectacularly inefficient. And unless you are naturally talented it is also, arguably, a waste of energy and time.

One of the problems with learning to ride is that horse riding itself has a long and distinguished history: it carries the burden of tradition. As with all traditions, some commonly held beliefs and practices are more of a hindrance than a help. Nevertheless they are all woven indiscriminately into the fabric of convention, leaving today's rider to decide which

of these conventions is dictated by history (such as always mounting from the near side, to avoid tripping over one's sword) and which is dictated by common sense (such as always mounting from a block, to avoid hauling on the horse's withers and damaging his spine).

What complicates matters is the fact that the skill of horse riding is taught, first and foremost, by the use of verbal commands, and through the passage of time the meaning of some phrases has become blurred. Other phrases are recent imports, and they are not even proper English! When you listen to the encrypted messages that fly around the arena, it is sometimes a wonder that anyone learns to ride. 'Off the leg', 'out through the shoulder', 'more off the hocks', 'more onto his hocks', 'more impulsion', 'less impulsion', 'heels down, shoulders back, hands together'… How? More importantly, *why*? Gifted teachers may inspire a pupil to make the right move at the right time. A gifted pupil may instinctively make the right move at the right time. But I remember watching an advanced dressage horse being asked to perform a walk pirouette, with a transition to canter down the centre line, under the eagle eye of an Olympic trainer. Twenty times he had to repeat the exercise, and twenty times he almost came to grief over his own front legs because of faulty timing on the part of the rider. No amount of verbal instruction could improve the situation. In the end, the exercise was abandoned.

As much as we try to do the right thing by our horses, it is inevitable that we should sometimes be drawn to riding techniques that are flawed (in that they either cause bad balance or interfere with natural balance). These techniques are often responsible for tension, and tension is always the precursor of strain. Have we any means of detecting tension before it causes lasting damage? Well, long before the horse shows clinical symptoms of strain he usually shows signs of tension – in his neck.

There have been a number of occasions when, as a veterinary surgeon, I have had to refer horses with severely restricted neck movements for specialist investigation. Yet, paradoxically, most of these horses came back with a diagnosis of disease in the hock, stifle, or sacroiliac joint. It was hard to reconcile the clinical diagnosis with the symptoms, particularly as it was the neck symptoms that had also caught the attention of trainers or physiotherapists. The answer is to be found not in veterinary books but in the works of the great classical riders of the past. Writing in the first half of the 19th century, François Baucher (a Frenchman of humble origins who became an authority on schooling techniques through the medium of the circus!), said: 'The head and neck of the horse are at once the rudder and compass of the rider ... there can be no elegance, no ease of the whole, when these two parts are stiff.' (*New Method of Horsemanship*, *see* Bibliography.)

In a note on horses that present difficulties for the rider owing to their conformation (for example, horses with a low croup or high withers), Baucher writes:

> ...we are obliged, in order to render his [the horse's] movements uniform, to lower his neck so that the kind of lever it represents may serve to lighten his hind parts from the weight with which they are overburdened.

He summarizes by saying:

> From the time I first noticed the powerful influence that the stiffness of the neck exercises on the whole mechanism of the horse, I attentively sought the means to remedy it.

Baucher's observations, as well as his means, are still worthy of our attention today. His message is taken up by General Decarpentry, a French horseman of the early 20th century, who puts the role of the neck in riding in a more obviously anatomical context:

> Lifting the neck without a Ramener [term for flexion of the head at the poll] causes the

muscles above the neck to slacken, and their slackening is communicated to the rest of the spine, which tends to collapse. In this manner, it diminishes the elasticity of the whole of the spinal column, limits the play of the hind legs, and considerably reduces their ability to engage under the mass.
>
> *Academic Equitation*, 1949

If based only on the observations of these two great horsemen, we must conclude that, since the horse is probably not inclined to use his neck to his own disadvantage, it must be we riders that are responsible for compromising the correct use of the horse's neck. Our interference leads to problems that later manifest themselves, clinically, at the other end of the horse's body. This biomechanical relationship is doubly underlined by the American dressage rider, Paul Belasik, in his discussion of the outside rein:

> Never does it [the outside rein] take an active role and actually bend the neck. This will only succeed in eventually disconnecting the neck from the horse's body and lead to a rubbery neck in front of the withers and a stiff body behind the withers – instead of a flexible body and a solidly connected neck, i.e., the horse moving in one piece.
>
> *Exploring Dressage Technique*, 1994

But as if to throw a spanner in the biomechanical works, enter Western rider Pat Parelli and his 'Natural Horse-Man-Ship'. Parelli is a remarkable horseman. Anybody who can guide a horse over obstacles, or work the horse through his instinctive fears, without recourse to gadgets, intimidation, or even a saddle and bridle – as he does – must qualify for the epithet 'remarkable'. What Parelli has also done is to set out a clear code of human conduct towards the horse, which enables riders to explore facets of human–horse interaction that are not on the agenda of conventional riding instruction. He calls this approach Natural Horse-Man-Ship.

In his outline of philosophy, he differentiates between human behaviour that is normal and that which is natural. Natural behaviour is instinctive, and allows us to be creative and individual; normal behaviour is conditioned, and makes us unimaginative and conformist. But what about the horse?

Parelli's system of teaching humans to become natural horsemen is actually based on the observation that the behaviour of horses is remarkably 'normal'. Horses want to conform. Whatever the task set by the human (for example, climbing onto a block or following an ATV across an open field), if the preparatory stimuli are well established the horse can be relied upon to respond consistently. If this were not the case it would be impossible for anyone to devise a systematic form of learning, natural or otherwise.

The dilemma presented by the Parelli system is that while it gives emotional security to the human (in handling his horse) it is often at the expense of the anatomical security of the horse. For example, a typical Parelli-ism is: 'Anybody can turn a horse on; can you turn him off?' (*Natural Horse-Man-Ship*, 1993.) As a method of stopping the horse – should he move off on his own or get out of control – the rider is told to run his hand down the lead rope or rein, draw the hand to the rider's thigh, and hold the neck in lateral flexion for up to thirty seconds. At a walking pace this is not unduly stressful. But at a fast trot, canter or gallop, this is a severe test of the connective tissues (fascia and ligaments) deep beneath the horse's shoulder blades, and the muscles at the junction of the neck and the thoracic spine. In the American Quarter Horse, this movement can probably be absorbed by the conformationally powerful muscular sling around the front of the chest. However, 'lateral flexion of the neck to disengage the quarters' is equivalent to jack-knifing the horse's body. How natural is that?

While there are several aspects of Parelli's method that put the horse at a biomechanical disadvantage, it has to be said that there are many aspects of his horsemanship that he shares with the old masters:

> Your attitude towards your horse should be a just one. In other words you should cause your ideas to be your horse's ideas, but understand what his ideas are first.
> Parelli, *Natural Horse-Man-Ship*, 1993

> But, admitting that the horse is less intelligent than you are, does it not behove you to use this intelligence … to make him understand what it is you want of him?"
> Baucher, *Dialogues on Equitation*, 1835

Almost two hundred years separate these two quotations, but horsemen everywhere (and not just those of the 'natural' persuasion) should take note of their common sentiment. In fact, it should probably be written large on the walls of all our tack rooms.

BACK TO BASICS

In the 20th century, the horse witnessed a great many changes brought about by world wars, men flying to the moon, the dawn of the dot-com era. He almost witnessed his own demise. But suddenly his star is in the ascendant, and the art of horsemanship has become a boom industry. The business of riding has been given a modern makeover. It now comes with a sort of quality-control label that reads 'Made in the 21st century'. So where does this leave the horseman?

As riders we cannot step outside our own skins. We cannot ignore the world around us or pretend that our lifestyles, our sense of pace and pressure, do not exist every time we climb into the saddle. However absorbed we become in the act of riding, we are nevertheless mentally the product of an 'on demand' society, and this affects our expectation of the horse.

It is not that long ago in the history of human evolution that horse transport was as fast as transport got. Measured against that,

The horse is not a machine…

any form of equestrian sport was an expression of ultimate power and control. Now we have cruise control, satellite navigation, and hundreds of horsepower from other sources at our disposal. If the horse was once high-tech, his human is now hyper-tech, and that has shifted the goalposts of riding.

At present there is an unhealthy tendency to pigeonhole riding techniques: 'natural', 'classical', 'competitive', Western, British, the world according to… whichever trainer is flavour of the month. The long-distance riders 'do' dressage out of season, the showjumpers and the eventers use flatwork as a means to an end, but it's only a few, in any branch of the sport, that have a true sense of holism.

...nor is he computer operated.

To prevent some of the disappointments that are the inevitable result of fragmentary training techniques, perhaps we should stop viewing the horse as so many pieces of a jigsaw puzzle spread out over a table. The pieces can be interlocked to form a complete picture, but only if we don't lose sight of the basic structures, and this means going back to basics.

If we peel back some of the veneers that riding has acquired even in the short space of this new millennium, we can begin to see what riding means – so to speak – from the horse's point of view. In fact, after centuries of horsemanship, it's still the best way to learn to ride: knowing how best to use the anatomy of the horse.

The horse is a living being whose body is powered by muscles and whose movements are organized by a brain. Nevertheless, these movements are mechanically defined by the shapes and fixtures of the joints.

GLOSSARY

Many books on riding begin with a diagram of the horse's anatomy. This provides the reader with points of reference for any terms later used in the text. However, we have to ask ourselves exactly which details of the horse's anatomy are really relevant to the rider's understanding of his skill. Is it better to know, for example, the location of the tuber coxae or the point of the hock, or the names of the superficial muscles? Or is it more appropriate to know how these features are joined together so that the body can move as a single integrated structure?

This glossary (numbers correspond to the illustration on page 18) contains a list of anatomical features that are constantly referred to in the text. They are structures of vital importance to the rider because they are directly affected by the rider's actions. For example, a horse may tear his suspensory apparatus as a result of a fast gallop on hard ground. The rider could be blamed for not taking care of the horse, but the rider did not, himself, physically intervene with the ligament: the horse could have sustained the same injury on his own. However, when it comes to pain over the poll, an aching jaw, tension through the withers, sacroiliac strain, or soreness in the back, the responsibility does lie with the rider. It may be that nothing has actually ruptured, but that does not mean to say that vital structures remain intact or that the horse is not without pain.

The main focus of this glossary is the connective tissues: the ligaments, tendons, and fascia. These are the recipients of huge muscular forces, and the means by which the power of the horse's muscles is transferred to the skeleton. Connective tissue supports the whole body like a complex web of stockings and suspenders. It's strong but not indestructible. It's part of the art of riding to respect the integrity of this web. After all, no one wants holes in their stockings.

1. Occiput.
At the back of the skull, this is the point of attachment for the nuchal ligament. This is arguably the most important point of concentrated muscle power on the skull since most of the muscles along the spine converge on the nuchal ligament or on its continuation, the supraspinous ligament.

2. Mastoid process.
On this small area of bone at the side of the skull converge several long neck muscles (a branch of the longissimus muscle, the brachiocephalic muscle, and part of the splenius muscle). It is the second focal point for the balancing powers of the neck. It is also the focus of muscular tension that can have a far-reaching effect – as far as the toes of the front feet.

3. Tuberosity of the lower jaw.
This is the place of insertion for the sternomandibularis muscle, and the third point of concentrated muscle power, this time from the underside of the neck.

4. Nuchal/supraspinous ligament.
This double ligament spans the entire spine, attaching itself to the tops of the dorsal spinous processes as far as the hindquarters. The large and small back muscles, and the fascias, which wrap round much of the body, attach to this ligament. Its role in giving support to the spine is unmistakable.

5. Fan-like ligamentous attachments from the nuchal ligament to the neck bones.
The last neck vertebrae depend for much of their security on these strap-like ligaments. Because this area is deep under the shoulder muscles, it is fairly inaccessible to diagnosis. But strain of these ligaments undoubtedly occurs, especially after falls on the base of the neck.

6. Fascia spinocostotransversalis.
This is the hidden fascia that forms the real connection between the forelimbs and the

17

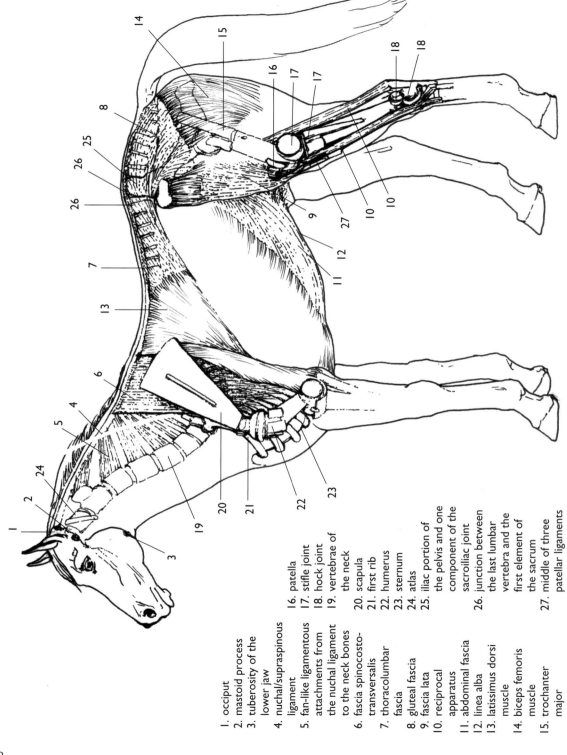

1. occiput
2. mastoid process
3. tuberosity of the lower jaw
4. nuchal/supraspinous ligament
5. fan-like ligamentous attachments from the nuchal ligament to the neck bones
6. fascia spinocosto-transversalis
7. thoracolumbar fascia
8. gluteal fascia
9. fascia lata
10. reciprocal apparatus
11. abdominal fascia
12. linea alba
13. latissimus dorsi muscle
14. biceps femoris muscle
15. trochanter major
16. patella
17. stifle joint
18. hock joint
19. vertebrae of the neck
20. scapula
21. first rib
22. humerus
23. sternum
24. atlas
25. iliac portion of the pelvis and one component of the sacroiliac joint
26. junction between the last lumbar vertebra and the first element of the sacrum
27. middle of three patellar ligaments

18

body wall. It serves as an area of attachment for some neck muscles; and most of the muscles that create the suspension of the forelimb (for example, the serratus ventralis muscle) adhere to its surface. It is attached to the nuchal ligament, and it consists of three layers, which spread out, like the sides of a tent, from the tops of the withers. The long back muscles pass between these layers on their way to the neck bones. For horses that work continually on the forehand, the strain to this fascia is immeasurable.

7. Thoracolumbar fascia.
This wraps around the lumbar muscles and defines the shape of the loins. It serves as an area of attachment for the latissimus dorsi muscle, whose prime function is to prevent the spine from buckling when the horse loads the front leg during a stride. This fascia leads into the fascia over the rump.

8. Gluteal fascia.
The most powerful muscles of the horse's body are attached to this fascia (for example, the biceps femoris muscle). It plays an important role in the transmission of power from the hindquarters to the back.

9. Fascia lata.
This fascia wraps itself round the quadriceps muscles and continues down the hind leg and around the stifle. It is by means of the fascia lata, and its extension, the fascia cruris, that the stifle joint is moved – since the thigh muscles insert on fascia rather than on bone.

10. Reciprocal apparatus.
A system of two modified muscles connect the stifle joint to the hock joint. There is further connection down the long tendons to the fetlock (not shown). These three joints are inextricably linked in flexion and extension, but the coupling mechanism can be put under severe strain if the horse is unable to lift his body and bring these joints underneath him as a single functional unit.

11 and 12. Abdominal fascia and linea alba.
Traction along this fascia and its midline connection, the linea alba, reinforces the traction along the top of the back.

13. Latissimus dorsi muscle.

14. Biceps femoris muscle.

15. Trochanter major.
A lever-like structure on the femur bone. It is the place of insertion of the gluteus medius muscle, which extends the hip joint, but also pushes the body forwards during the stance phase of the hind-limb stride.

16. Patella.

17. Stifle joint.

18. Hock joint.

19. Vertebrae of the neck.

20. Scapula.

21. First rib.

22. Humerus.

23. Sternum.

24. Atlas.
First neck bone.

25. Iliac portion of the pelvis and one component of the sacroiliac joint.

26. Junction between the last lumbar vertebrae and the first element of the sacrum.

27. Middle of three patellar ligaments.
These are an integral part of the stifle mechanism, and connect the quadriceps muscles to the tibial crest. This transmission is linked to that of the reciprocal apparatus.

1 Anatomy Revisited: the Horse

Muscle is elastic; fascia is plastic.
      Thomas W. Myers, *Anatomy Trains*, 2001

The above quotation is taken from an innovative book, written by the American Rolf practitioner Thomas Myers. On the face of it, his could be just another book on manipulative therapy for humans or, as it's now called, bodyworking. However, what makes this book special is that its author challenges our commonly held view that muscles and bones are the star attraction in any performance of movement. Instead he relegates these to the chorus line and brings into the limelight the lesser known player, the connective tissue. According to Myers, the real celebrity of movement is a structure called the fascia. (As yet, a similar book for horses does not exist so the one by Myers will have to act as a role model.)

RAILWAY TRACKS

Fascia is part of an all-embracing network of tissue that spreads throughout the whole body, supporting the internal organs and the musculoskeletal system. Externally this network can be differentiated into tendons, ligaments, cartilage, the fine mesh that surrounds large and small bundles of muscle fibre, and the fascia. Essentially, these structures are all made of collagen, which is interspersed with substances such as proteoglycans or chondroitin sulphate. This makes each structure biomechanically suitable for its specific location. Myers's analogy is that this network of connective tissue is like a system of railway lines (hence the title,

Anatomy Trains). It runs through the whole locomotor apparatus, enabling us – and the horse – to move as a single integrated unit.

However, we know that connective tissue is not, by itself, responsible for movement. Movement is initiated when a muscle receives an electrical signal from a motor nerve. This causes the muscle to contract, changing the position of the bone on which the muscle inserts. If muscles provide the power, what is the function of fascia?

Let's imagine that we can remove the skin from the horse's body. What sort of structures do you see just below the surface? In some places, such as the neck and upper limbs, there are muscles. In the lower limbs, there are tendons and ligaments. But over the loins, under the belly, over the quarters, and around the thighs, there are broad swathes of tissue that are obviously not muscular. Muscles are there, of course, but they are not immediately visible. They are packaged, and it's the packaging that is important.

The silvery, glistening sheets of tissue that envelope so much of the horse's body are called fascia. Each 'sheet' is named after its particular location (for example, gluteal, thoracolumbar, or spinocostotransversal), and each sheet usually consists of more than one layer. These layers extend between different muscles, or groups of muscles, separating them from one another and enabling each muscle or muscle group to move independently of its neighbour.

The point about fascia is that, unlike muscle, it is not a self-contained unit: it literally has a great many fingers in a great many pies. Although the fibres undergo some structural modifications, fundamentally we can think of fascia as having multiple strands, which spread through the horse's muscles to form strong connections with the tendons on the other side. Sometimes these strands insert directly onto the ligaments of the joints.

This means that whenever a muscle works it changes not only the action of its tendon but the tension across a fascia. What is more, we can follow direct lines of connective tissue from one end of the body to the other. For example, we can follow a line from the lumbar fascia, down through the latissimus dorsi muscle to its connection with the tensor fascia antibrachii muscle, through the fascia of the forearm, and from here – via the deep digital flexor muscle and tendon – to the sole of the foot. Similarly, we can follow a line from the supraspinous ligament and the gluteal fascia, through the biceps femoris muscle to the crural fascia around the stifle, and from here via the middle patellar ligament, reciprocal apparatus and common extensor tendon, to the hind toe.

This is what Myers means by 'anatomy trains': specific pathways of movement that are maintained not by muscles but by continuous 'tracks' of connective tissue. The significance is (to continue the analogy) that derailments can occur – through injury, for example. In such cases, movement has to be re-routed. This leads to a pattern of compensation, which can put a considerable strain on the connective tissue network.

Let's consider the following statement, taken from the same book:

> Stretched, a muscle will attempt to recoil back to its resting length. Stretch a fascia quickly and it will tear (the most frequent form of connective tissue injury). If the stretch is applied slowly enough, it will deform plastically: it will change its length and retain that change.

Immediately we can see that this has enormous implications in horse riding. It is often said that the horse is not meant to be ridden because he is not designed to carry weight on his back. This is only a half-truth. It's not weight, per se, that is bad for the horse: it's the capacity of weight to hold up the train of movement. Weight, as applied to riding, means everything from the fit of the saddle and bridle to the touch of the spur, the softness of the hand, and even the way the rider breathes.

If we look at the position of the fascial connections, under the horse's shoulders, across his back, around his entire hindquarters, and, if we consider that it is the presence of fascia that enables the horse to gather himself together, lighten the forehand, and transfer his bodyweight onto the hind limbs, we can begin to imagine the extent to which the rider's presence can affect this train of movement. The rider has the capacity to directly interfere with the integrity of the fascia, and this should make us aware of the enormous responsibility that lies with, for example, the fit of the saddle, the 'depth' of the rider's seat and the position of his legs.

RAILWAY STATIONS

If tendons, ligaments, and fascia, are the connective tissue tracks along which movement travels, then the joints must be the stations. Movement can either pass through the stations without stopping, or it can pause momentarily, or it can halt altogether. This is especially significant for riding because many of the horse's joints have, to all intents and purposes, only a single axis of movement, like a hinge. However big they are – the stifle joint or the carpus, for example – they are not designed to rotate or swivel significantly. Yet, in riding we ask the horse to perform twists and turns, and to move laterally.

The way in which the horse moves laterally is limited by the shape of his joints. The mechanism that enables the horse to move sideways consists of a complicated sequence of muscle actions, but its potential is arguably enhanced by the stretchiness (plasticity) of the fascia. The same is true of bending, pirouetting, making flying changes, jumping – in fact almost everything that goes beyond simply walking forwards.

If we take into account what this means to the body at microscopic level, we can begin to see the possible source of many chronic lamenesses and back problems. As Thomas Myers puts it:

> Stress going through a material deforms the material, thereby 'stretching' the bonds between the molecules. This creates a slight electric flow known as a piezo- (pressure) electric charge. This can be 'read' by the cells in the vicinity of the charge, and the connective tissue cells are capable of responding by augmenting, reducing, or changing the intercellular elements in the area.

If you are now thinking of ring bone, side bone, lower joint disease, or of regular visits from the chiropractor to straighten the atlas bone, unblock the withers, and realign the pelvis, you are probably on the right lines.

The biomechanical versatility of the horse's musculoskeletal system is unique. But the only way the horse can have flexibility as well as strength is by combining the driving power of the muscles with the restraining power of the connective tissues. In this way the horse's body can absorb the impact of his strides as well as keep his balance under the influence of the rider. Used in the right way, connective tissue is efficient and energy saving. Used in the wrong way it has the capacity to interrupt the flow of movement, and eventually break down.

Put simply, if we, as riders, ignore the role of the connective tissues in movement we ultimately sacrifice the healthy structure of the joints. Fascia is our ally: it is the key to a railway that works.

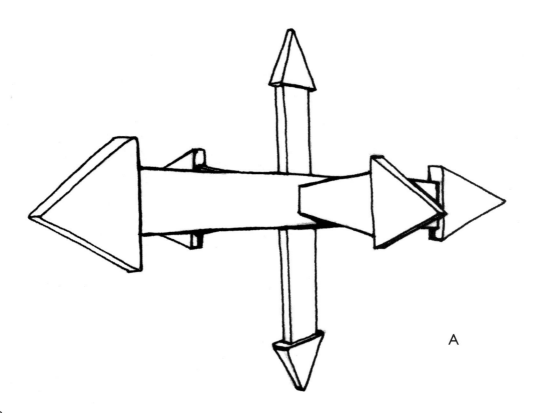

A

In his book, *Natural Horse-Man-Ship*, Western rider Pat Parelli describes the horse as having six directions of movement: forwards, backwards, sideways (left and right), upwards, and downwards. As many riders now use the Parelli method of training horses, this statement needs some clarification.

For the purposes of teaching, Parelli's 'six directions' may be a reasonable simplification. But they are in danger of being an oversimplification because they give us false expectations of the horse's movements. They are a bit too literal, and they also make us think that the horse can carry out movements in these six directions with equal ease.

In reality, the deciding factor is the shape of the horse's joints. They are designed for the horse to move forwards, and the sides of the joints (laterally and medially) are held in place by ligaments. This virtually guards against any serious movement sideways. By virtue of the action of certain muscles (adductors and abductors) the horse can draw the limbs both towards and away from the long axis of his body. But this capacity is not very great when one compares it to the muscles that propel the horse forwards.

Rather than moving sideways, we should think of the horse as moving obliquely. And he does this by ingenious combination of muscle lift and connective tissue support. The greater the emphasis on side-to-side movement – and yes, horses have been taught to line-dance – the greater the pressure on the ligaments.

In the context of riding, the upward and downward movements are usually part of the overall trend forwards. They may, temporarily, involve the whole body, but it is far more usual for them to involve one part of the body only. Likewise, backwards is, or should be, only a transitional movement for the purpose of gathering the horse together (or gathering his attention). If it is not integrated into a general move forwards, it can pose a serious threat to less well-supported areas of the spine. The horse gets mechanically 'stuck' in reverse.

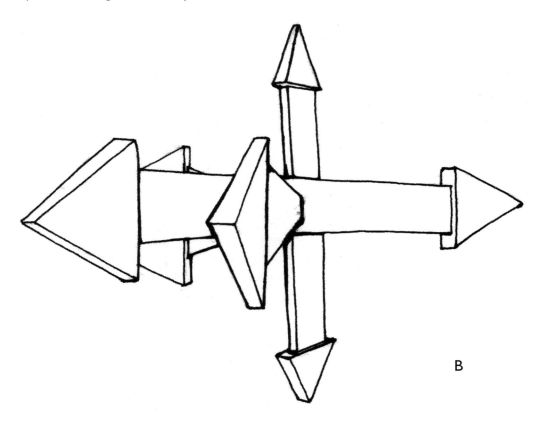

B

Let's look at the directions of movement in more detail. The horse's forward movement is unambiguous: from a racing gallop (A) to ambling round the field (B), the direction is unmistakable.

A

B

The movement backwards is altogether ambiguous. In horse A there is nothing in the footfall or the posture to characterize this as a rein-back: just the slight tension through the neck and the position of the ears might give the game away.

On the other hand, horse B does suggest a backward move. At the very least he is resisting going forwards. However, he could still go upwards, or, since the left forefoot is planted laterally, head off sideways.

In horse A the back is braced and the weight is bearing onto the hock and hind fetlock. The horse then has to lift himself through the withers and base of the neck. The movement needs great care – and great respect on the part of the rider.

In horse B the neck is hollow and the lumbar spine is compressed. He is shunting himself backwards and has to tense the abdominal muscles in order to get the feet off the ground. If this movement were repeated too often in this way, it would certainly produce a repetitive-strain type injury – possibly in the fascia beneath the shoulder blades.

The upward movement is almost as unambiguous as forward – with which it is usually combined.

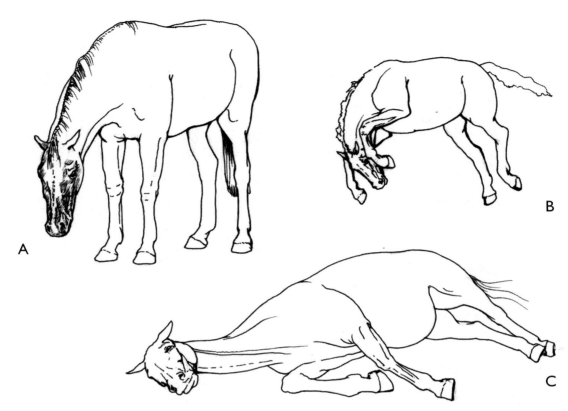

Downwards is the most ambiguous of movements. It is usually part of a combination of movements. For example, downwards can be integrated into an expression of submission, of temper, or of sheer frustration. The horse flat out on the ground (C) had to get down, but from this position the only way to go is up. Therefore, downwards is perhaps best described as a mode. Downwards mode can be subtle and not instantly recognizable.

A horse that is apparently working on the bit, that is 'tracking up', and apparently compliant, may be in downward mode. In horse D the muscle line above the eyebrow and the line of the cheekbone indicate that although he is trying to look upwards and forwards his vision is being directed downwards, just in front of his feet.

We have to ask ourselves whether a horse would carry himself in this way if he were not being ridden or lunged.

The capacity of the horse to move sideways is relatively limited. There are only a few muscles that can draw the limb towards or away from the long axis of the body, and the most significant of these are in the hindquarters.

By virtue of their shape, the hip and shoulder joints allow a small amount of rotational movement. But the majority of the surrounding muscles are, nevertheless, flexors and extensors producing a forward movement. The only joint with a built-in swivel action is the hock. The stifle allows for sideways movement because it is strapped into a tight stocking of connective tissue, the crural fascia.

In reality, sideways is a combination of forwards (or backwards) and upwards: the horse moves obliquely rather than literally sideways. To do so he has to brace the muscles of the upper body and neck. But exactly how he does this depends on the situation: for example, horse B does it as part of a schooling exercise; horse C does it as part of a flight or fight response.

When the sideways movement is carried to extremes as, for example, in branches of Western riding, or in bull-fighting, the combined turning power of the thigh, back and neck muscles spirals through the hocks and hind fetlocks to the pasterns.

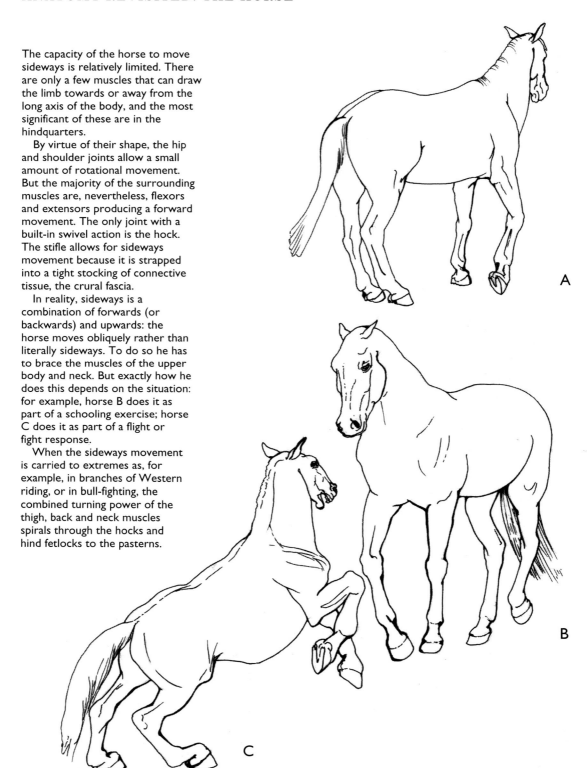

28

The natural movements of the horse's limbs are defined by the shape of the joints. In horses whose conformation permits it, these movements can be enhanced, but this does not alter the basic parameters set by joint shape. If we depict the joints as simple mechanical shapes, we can double-check whether the joints are really capable of matching our (riders') expectations of them.

Figure A shows the mechanical shapes in their correct order. The shoulder has some capacity to swivel, as do the pastern and coffin joints. But the shoulder joint is retained by the tendons of the shoulder muscles, and the joints of the foot are held in alignment by a dense strapping of ligaments. The shapes chosen are an approximation of the joints' biomechanical function (ball and socket, barrel hinge). They simply serve to make the movement of each joint clear – at a glance.

Let's exchange the two shapes of the shoulder and elbow joints, as in figure B. We can see that we might *think* this is how the forelimb moves, but it is not a correct interpretation. It becomes even further from the truth if we depict the knee (carpus) and fetlock as being able to rotate (C) – which of course they can't.

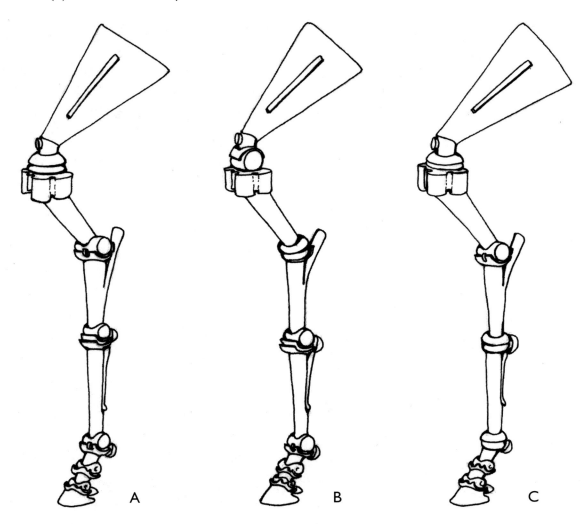

A   B   C

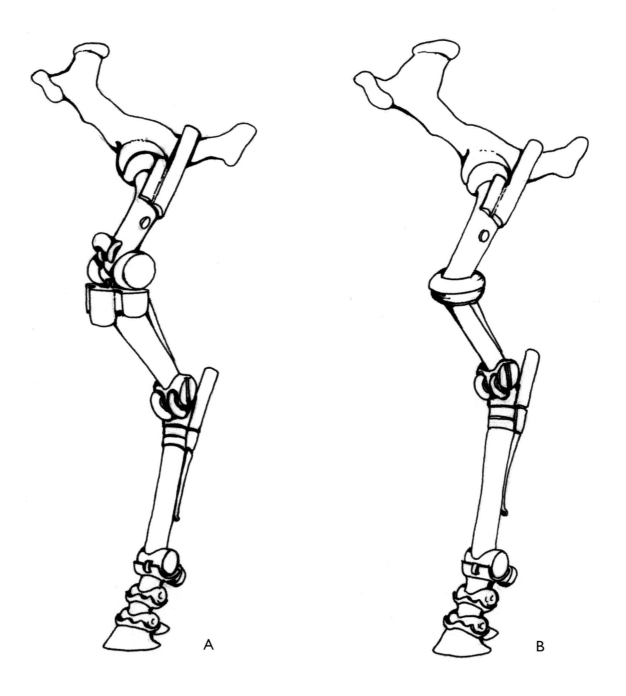

A

B

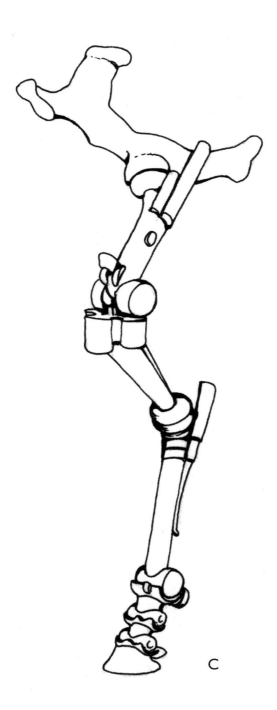

C

Misconceptions become even more bizarre when we apply the same principle to the joints of the hind limb. Figure A shows the joints in their correct order. The hip is a ball-and-socket joint. But the presence of the huge lever, called the trochanter major, belies the fact that the main direction of movement is forwards (and backwards). The stifle allows the horse 'to turn on a sixpence', like a steam roller turning on a precipice, but still there are structures in place (for example the patella mechanism) that highlight the function of this joint as a simple hinge.

The screw-like shape of the hock prevents the lower limb from hitting the horse's belly as the limb flexes, but it is still fundamentally a hinge (although the screw-like properties come into their own at the half pass, the pirouette and in barrel racing).

It is clear, then, that if in our minds we start to change the shapes of the joints about – put a ball-and-socket at the stifle (B) or at the hock (C) – our expectations as riders exceed the functional reality.

31

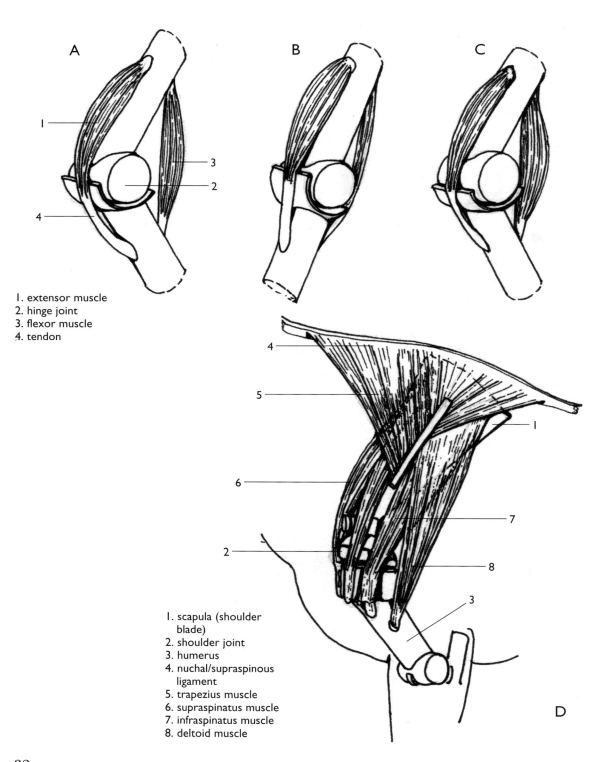

A

B

C

1. extensor muscle
2. hinge joint
3. flexor muscle
4. tendon

1. scapula (shoulder
   blade)
2. shoulder joint
3. humerus
4. nuchal/supraspinous
   ligament
5. trapezius muscle
6. supraspinatus muscle
7. infraspinatus muscle
8. deltoid muscle

D

Movement is produced by the action of muscles on bones. The muscle has a place of origin and a place of insertion. Each muscle or muscle group has an antagonistic partner: one muscle serves to open a joint, the other to close it again (figures A, B, C).

Joints with a hinge mechanism (most joints in the horse's limbs) are held in alignment by ligaments placed on either side (laterally and medially). The ligaments are often paired, of slightly different lengths, and insert at different places on the side of the joint. This means that once a joint has reached a certain angle, the muscle has to overcome the natural resistance from the ligaments in order to move the joint any further. It also means that the ligaments have a natural tendency to snap the joint shut. This saves on muscle power.

No muscle works in isolation. This can be seen in figures D (shoulder), E (stifle and hock), and F (hip).

The shoulder joint (D) cannot be moved without the influence of the trapezius muscle, which originates along the nuchal/supraspinous ligament. This ligament is attached to the withers and continues along the top of the spine to the quarters.

The hock (E) cannot move without influencing the stifle.

The muscles flex and extend the hip joint (F). However, because of the position of the gluteus medius muscle, spanning the gap diagonally between the trochanter major and the pelvis, this muscle can also pull the leg outwards. The muscles on the medial (inner) side of the limb pull the thigh bone towards the body.

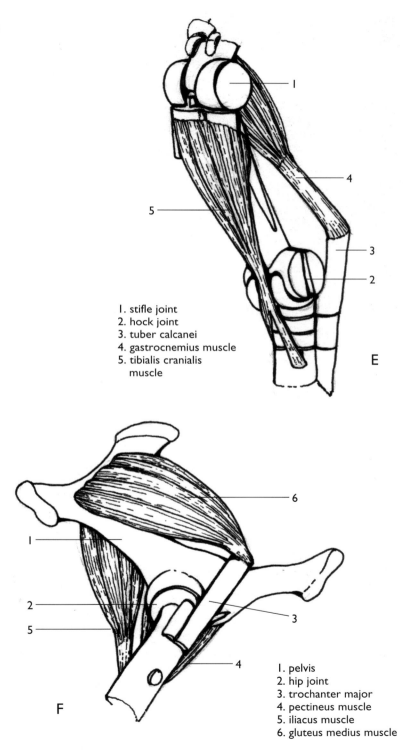

1. stifle joint
2. hock joint
3. tuber calcanei
4. gastrocnemius muscle
5. tibialis cranialis muscle

E

1. pelvis
2. hip joint
3. trochanter major
4. pectineus muscle
5. iliacus muscle
6. gluteus medius muscle

F

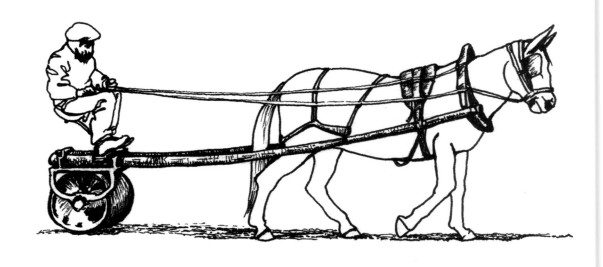

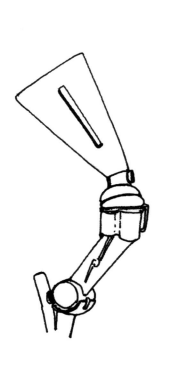

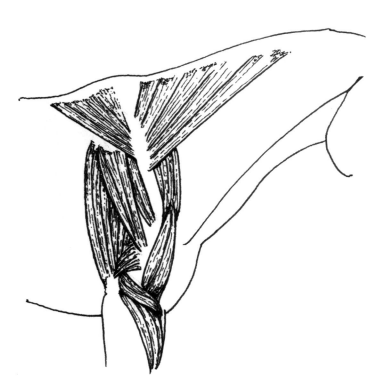

The role of connective tissue
in movement.

In his book *Anatomy Trains*, Thomas
Myers likens the function of
connective tissue to railway tracks.
In order to give a sense of structure
as well as function, we can use the
analogy of the horse-drawn vehicle.

Imagine that the mule is the
muscle, and the farmer with his
implement is the bone, or skeleton.
Without the harness and shafts, the
pulling power of the mule would be
of little use. It is clear that the mule
needs some means of attachment
to the agricultural implement.

Like the mule, the muscles
literally have to be harnessed. The
harness is provided by connective
tissue: tendons, ligaments and,
most importantly, fascia.

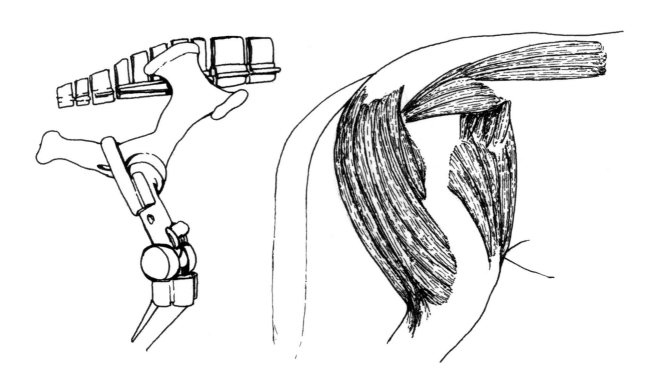

Muscle power is harnessed to the skeleton by means of strong connective tissue. It threads its way between the muscle fibres, and envelops the whole muscle (not shown here), helping to give each muscle its distinctive shape.

These two diagrams are bird's-eye views of the forelimb (A) and hind limb (B), looking down from the shoulder and croup respectively. (It's the view we have when, for example, we are riding, or pulling the tail.)

The diagrams demonstrate that there is an uninterrupted pathway of connective tissue from the place we call the muscle's origin to the place of its insertion. Every muscle is anchored by means of a tendon, however short that tendon may be. A great many muscles have their origin and insertion not on bones but on broad sheets of connective tissue called fascia.

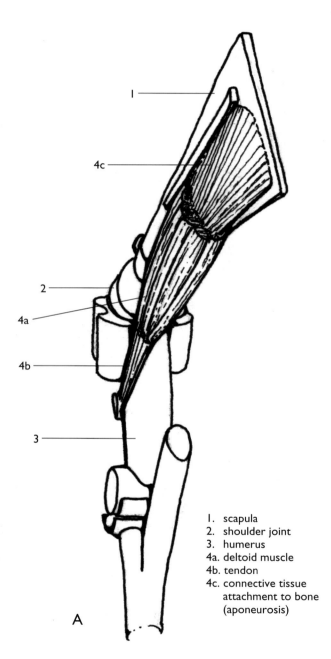

1. scapula
2. shoulder joint
3. humerus
4a. deltoid muscle
4b. tendon
4c. connective tissue attachment to bone (aponeurosis)

A

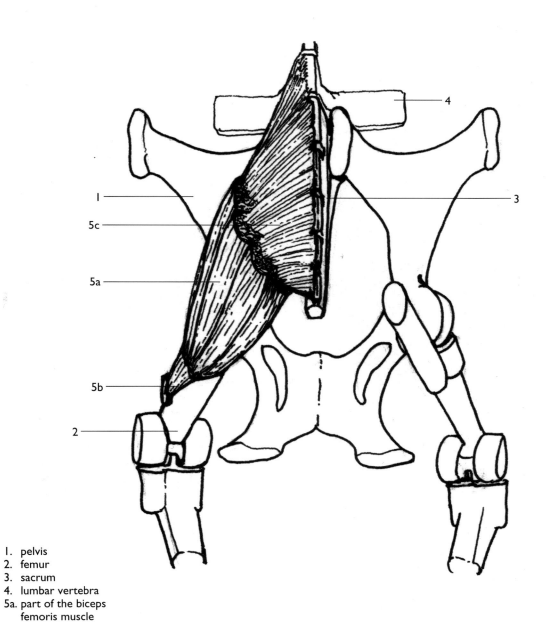

1. pelvis
2. femur
3. sacrum
4. lumbar vertebra
5a. part of the biceps
    femoris muscle
5b. tendon attachment
5c. connective tissue
    attachment to
    the bone

B

37

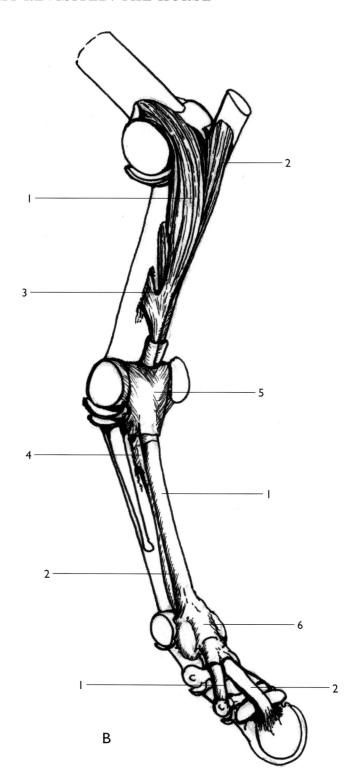

1. superficial digital
   flexor muscle
   and tendon
2. deep digital flexor
   muscle and tendon
3. superior check
   ligament
4. inferior check
   ligament
5. retinaculum
6. tendon sheath

B

The calibre of the muscles and their connective tissue harness varies from place to place around the body, just as a particular type of horse will be chosen to suit a particular vehicle (A).

In B, the foreleg of the horse is seen from the medial side and shows the superficial digital flexor muscle and tendon (1), and the deep digital flexor muscle and tendon (2).

Apart from their places of origin (humerus and olecranon) and insertion (pastern and pedal bone), the flexor muscles have connective tissue linkages to each other, to the bones via the superior (3) and the inferior (4) check ligaments, to the carpal joint via the retinaculum (5), and to the sesamoid bones and fetlock joint via the tendon sheath (6) and annular ligament.

By comparison with some other muscles in the horse's body, these muscles are not huge. But by a complex system of interconnections, the shafts and traces of connective tissue enable these muscles to flex the whole leg. What is more, in the stance phase of a stride, they help to stabilize the leg as it takes the full weight of the horse's body – and that of the rider.

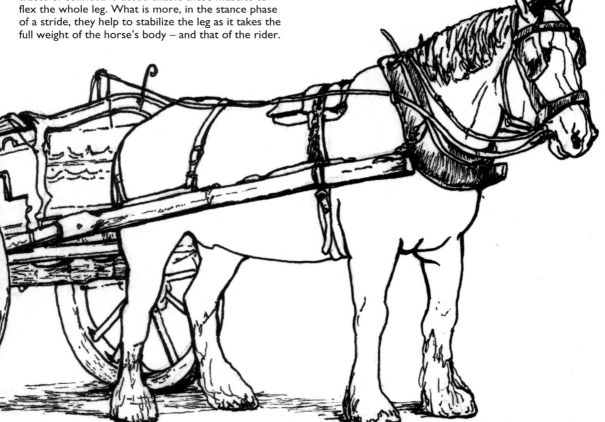

Chains of support.

Connective tissue linkages serve to coordinate a series of movements through different groups of muscles, like a number of horses harnessed in single file.

For example, as the swing phase of a stride changes to stance, strong connective tissue attachments serve to stabilize the leg, prevent the spine from buckling, and help to propel the body forwards.

One long chain of connective tissue stabilizers begins with the biceps muscle and its special extension feature (1), and the lacertus fibrosus (2). This connects with the extensor carpi radialis muscle (3), which inserts below the 'knee'. The extensor action is continued by the tendon of the common digital extensor muscle (4).

A second chain begins as far back as, the thoracolumbar fascia (5). This provides a broad area of insertion for the latissimus dorsi muscle (6), which has connective tissue links to the teres major (7) and tensor fascia antibrachi muscles (8), as well as the triceps muscle (not shown).

From the tensor fascia antibrachii muscle, there is a further chain of support down the medial side of the leg (as shown in the diagram on page 38).

As the horse moves onto his forehand, we can begin to see the enormous significance of the fascia. Its purpose is to help brace the horse's back during the transmission of power from the hindquarters.

If the horse works predominantly on the forehand, the fascia can help to brace the side of the chest and shoulder (through the latissimus dorsi muscle). It will do this until it has exhausted its reserve in 'stretchiness' (plasticity).

1. biceps muscle
2. lacertus fibrosus
   (the special extension
   feature of the biceps
   muscle)
3. extensor carpi
   radialis muscle
4. tendon of the
   common digital
   extensor muscle
5. thoracolumbar fascia
6. latissimus dorsi
   muscle
7. teres major
8. tensor fascia
   antibrachi muscles

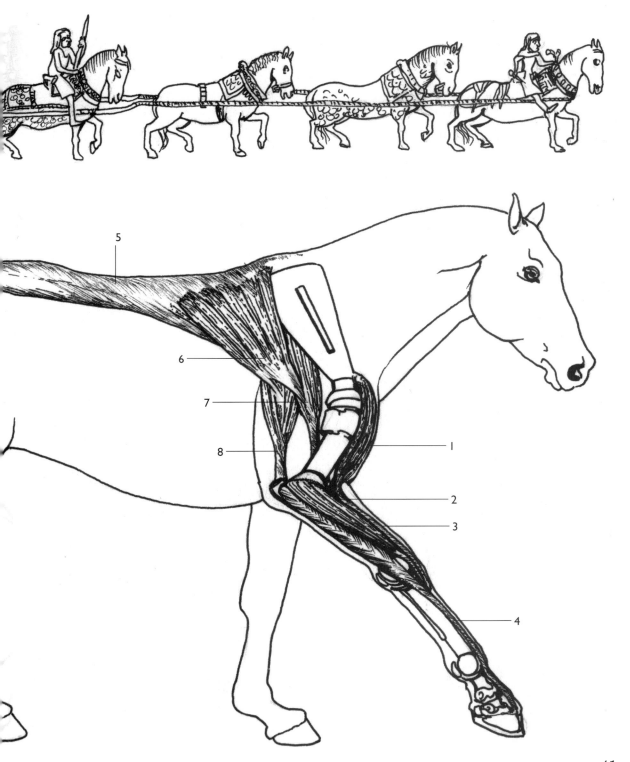

The incredible connective tissue harness of the hind leg: it exudes power like the harnessing of this Russian four-in-hand.

Almost none of the muscles of the hind leg inserts directly onto bones. Instead, they insert onto ligaments, broad areas of fascia, and specially reinforced areas of joint capsules (which double as ligaments).

In conjunction with the special design of the stifle and hock joints and the presence of the reciprocal apparatus, which operates the two joints in tandem, connective tissue is the 'last word' in energy efficiency. It strengthens the recoil of the muscles, enabling the hind limb to be a powerful springboard for the body, as well as an even more deadly weapon of defence.

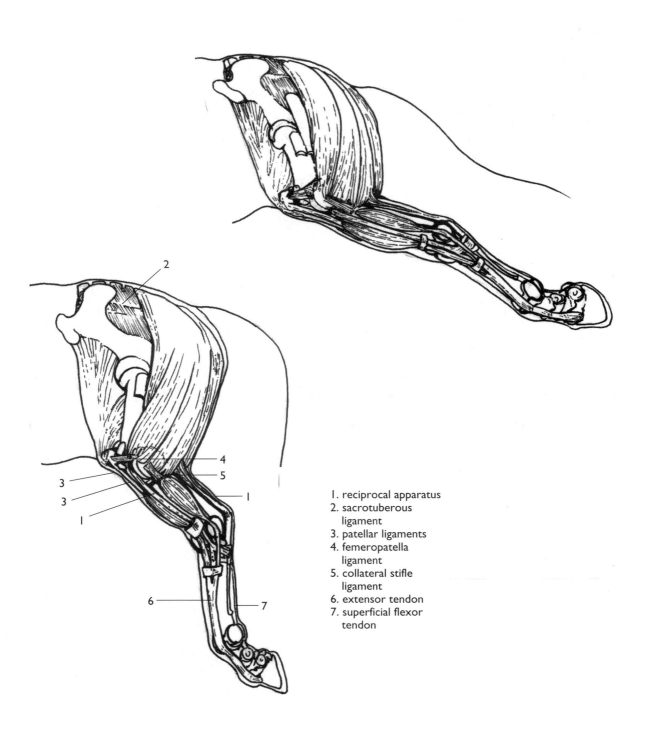

1. reciprocal apparatus
2. sacrotuberous
   ligament
3. patellar ligaments
4. femeropatella
   ligament
5. collateral stifle
   ligament
6. extensor tendon
7. superficial flexor
   tendon

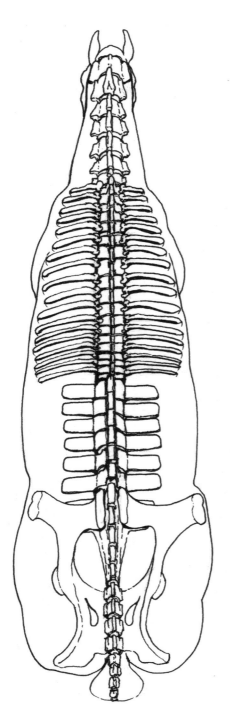

(*Left*) One of the reasons that connective tissue is so important to the rider is that it helps to protect the integrity of the horse's spine. The spinal column transmits the shifting weight of the body from limb to limb, whilst also carrying the weight of the rider. If the horse's movements are to remain fluent, without jarring, much depends on the alignment of the connective tissue straps, which hold the small interlocking joints of the spine in position. These are at risk if, because of inadequate fascia support, the horse's posture sags.

In this diagram, we are looking at the spine from above. (The many small joints have been omitted for clarity.)

(*Right*) At strategic points along the spine, there are junctions that are designed to be highly manoeuvrable. They are, to all intents and purposes, the real source of the horse's flexibility. For this reason, these junctions are less well supported by powerful musculature (than, say, the upper limbs or the lower back), and depend very significantly on ligamentous connections, and fascia. In fact, most of these junctions have few direct muscle connections, but are contained by a cross-bracing of muscle 'flyovers'.

For example, figure A shows that if the head is raised, it pushes the atlas bone (1) back, which forces the other neck bones down. This squashes the parotid (saliva) gland (2), and the trachea (airway) (3) – especially if the tongue (4) is drawn back (for example, to escape an uncomfortable bit, or hand).

Figure B shows that a similar compression occurs if the horse's neck is overbent. This time it affects the function of the long, ventral neck muscles.

If the head is drawn back (C), the area of the first rib (5), and the withers are pressed downwards. However, if the horse's head is just in front of the vertical, the poll is the highest point, and the neck muscles are flexed but not in traction (D), the horse can 'come up' through the withers, and the pressure on the throat and the area of the first rib are instantly relieved.

The different sections of the spine can be recognized by the changing shape of the dorsal vertebral processes (E). Whilst each section of the spine – cervical (6), thoracic (7), lumbar (8), and sacral (9) – has an identifiable, structural coherence, there is often an abrupt change of shape at the junctions between one section and the next. It is clear that, for this reason, fluent movement is paramount to protect these junctions from strain.

The muscles along the spine play an important part in posture as well as in movement. But they cannot, by themselves, be expected to perform these important functions as well as support the weight of the rider. On the contrary, this significant contribution to making riding possible is performed by the fascia.

(It is worth noting here, that the flexible junctions along the horse's spine are also areas where important nerve bundles are concentrated. Any mechanical stress that weakens these junctions must also have an effect on nerve transmission.)

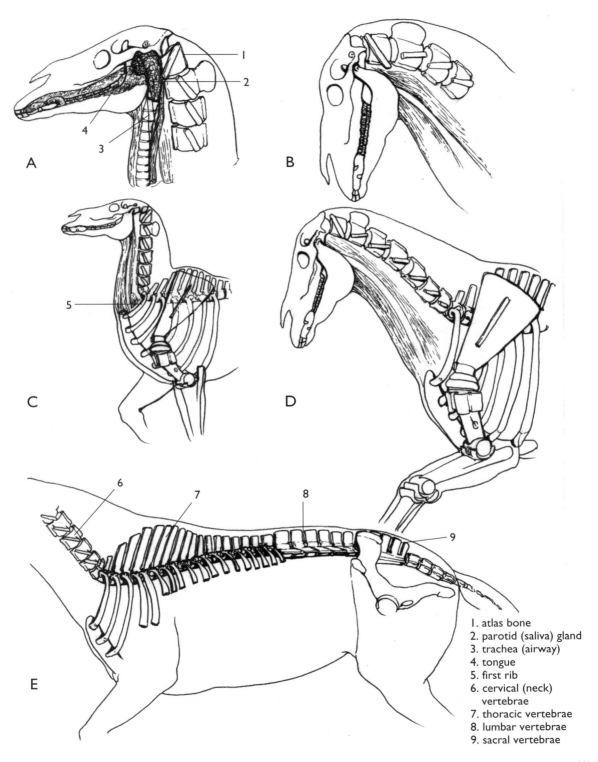

A

B

C

D

E

1. atlas bone
2. parotid (saliva) gland
3. trachea (airway)
4. tongue
5. first rib
6. cervical (neck)
   vertebrae
7. thoracic vertebrae
8. lumbar vertebrae
9. sacral vertebrae

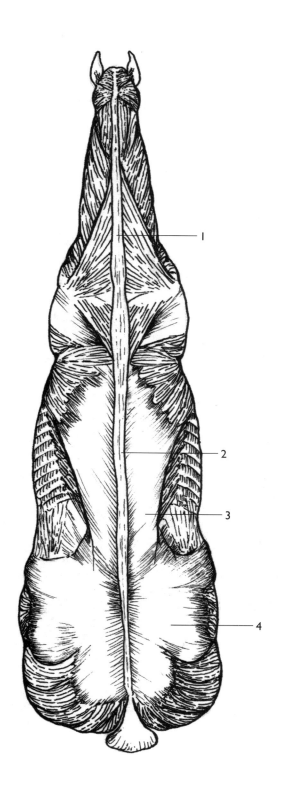

Looking at the horse from above, we can see that areas of the horse's back and hindquarters are encased in broad swathes of connective tissue (fascia). Here only the most superficial layer is shown, but in reality there are usually three layers which weave their way between groups of muscles.

The 'topline' is dominated by the feature of the nuchal/supraspinous ligament, a long tendon-like structure that attaches to much of the spine and to which many of the layers of fascia themselves attach.

As riders we rely on these connective tissue structures to bring unity and fluency to the horse's movements. We have to take care that the way we ride, or our choice of equipment, does not impede the fascia, and thereby isolate strategic areas of movement from the whole.

1. nuchal ligament
2. supraspinous ligament
3. thoracolumbar fascia
4. gluteal fascia

Not a view often seen by the rider – hopefully!

Fascia also plays an important role in supporting the abdomen and – as can be seen from this perspective – also the hind leg, especially in the region of the stifle.

However, in contrast to the abdomen, the underside of the chest depends on the active suspension of the pectoral muscles.

Although there are important areas of fascia between the shoulder blades, the front part of the chest, strengthened as it is by the construction of the ribcage, has no significant fascia, only muscles.

Whereas fascia responds to mechanical stress by stretching, muscles exhaust their elasticity if they are overworked. Tense pectoral muscles gradually lose their ability to cushion the forehand. The horse then depends on the inherent strength of the fascia (for example, between the shoulders), to prevent him from jarring.

This explains why lightness of the forehand is not only desirable but essential if the integrity of the structure is to be protected while carrying the weight of a rider. Lightness provides that all-important safety-net.

1. pectoral muscles
2. abdominal fascia
3. linea alba
4. inguinal ligament
5. fascia lata
6. fascia cruris

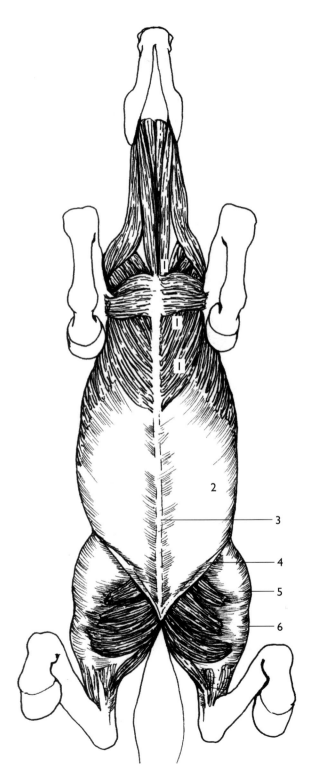

47

2 Great Expectations: the Rider

The successful horseman must make a study of his horse so that he may give lessons based on mutual understanding… which will enable the rider to solve a fundamental question, that of the ideal position which must be given to the horse according to the specific exercise in question.

Nuno Oliveira, *Reflections on Equestrian Art*, 1976

What, do you think, is the most popular advice given to riders today? Is it the classical 'deepen your seat', 'lengthen your leg', 'lighten your hand'? Or the old-fashioned 'sit up straight, shoulder blades together, chest out, stomach in, heels down' (said all in one breath)? Or the enigmatic 'Imagine that… you are holding two mugs of tea', '…you have an eye in the middle of your pelvis', or '…you have two pencils extending from your seat bones'? No. The most popular advice of today is that we should 'learn to think like a horse'.

Everybody's advocating it: behavioural therapists, 'natural horsemen', and, most recently, dressage trainers. On the face of it, it may seem harmless enough. It may even strike us as being particularly sensitive and humane. But is this advice really of any use? Do we do the horse any favours by imagining that we can put ourselves in his shoes?

Let's be clear about this: 'to think like a horse' is not the same as 'to understand how a horse thinks'. This is not just nit-picking. The difference is great – so great, in fact, that it spans millions of years of evolution.

We would probably all agree that, in the partnership between humans and horses, one partner has to be the leader and the other the follower. A leader is one who is the 'author' of a pattern of thoughts, for example, a task to be performed. The follower is one who accepts this 'authority' because it's a means of achieving this task. Of course the horse can take the lead (in that he can use his physical ingenuity and intuition to help the rider). But, at the end of the day, it's up to the human to maintain the authority: any other way is likely to be a compromise on safety.

Authority grows out of knowledge. In the case of horsemanship, it grows out of knowing what to expect of the horse's behaviour, and how this behaviour relates to movement. To learn this behaviour, we can either use the power of our imagination, and try to imitate it, or we can use the power of perception and try to study it, acknowledging that this behaviour is what it means to be a horse. The first way leads us to empathy. But the second way leads us to sympathy.

If we ride sympathetically, we feel for what motivates or repels the horse, and this prevents us from pushing him beyond his natural boundaries before he is ready. If we ride empathetically, we feel only these natural boundaries, and this means we may not push the horse at all. In fact, we may not even ride.

The major flaw with the idea of 'thinking like a horse' is that we can't – because we are mentally and physically too far removed, thanks to the process of evolution. It's not just our upright posture, though that's enough to change anybody's perspective. It's a matter of our ability to twist and turn our bodies – and to rotate our limbs. Whatever anybody may say, it's actually extraordinarily hard for an upright biped to imagine what it must be like to have four limbs attached to the body in such a way that they can only move forwards and backwards. It's even harder to imagine how these limbs work when they are combined with a spine that moves predominantly horizontally. We humans take the smallest rotational gesture for granted. Even if we get down on all fours, we have to spread our legs because they are too long. And we have to throw our heads back (in the 'startle' position), to see where we are going. The horse has none of these problems.

Nevertheless, it is the ability to do these things, the ability to move our bodies in a highly creative way, that enables us to ride the horse in the first place. We are the species that can abduct and adduct our limbs sufficiently to enable us to sit on the back of a horse. That's what makes us riders. Unfortunately, it is the same creativity that can technically prevent us from riding well.

To highlight the difference, let's imagine a horse wheeling round in a pirouette, and an ice-skater performing a spin. We can see that the two movements, though superficially similar, are carried out in very different ways. The horse has to brace his body while he pivots round on his feet; the ice-skater pivots by leading with the upper body in a spiral twist. The human brain has evolved to choreograph a wide range of rotational movements (such as those needed to tee off at golf, or to serve at tennis). This means that, in riding, we have to be careful not to move at cross purposes with the horse.

SHAPES AND SIZES

If you go into any livery yard, and look at the horses with their owners, it often seems that the most unlikely shapes and sizes are paired together. If only the riders could exchange horses, then the tall human would be with the tall horse, the short with the short, and so on. Nevertheless, the fact that the tall, lanky person has a small pony, and the short, stocky person has a huge horse, tells us something about the art of riding. It tells us that riding can be a matter of physical versatility.

The problem is that the scope of human movement makes riding instruction extremely difficult. Where is the correct seat, the most effective use of the leg, the best height for the hand? What if the horse is 16.3 hh. and the rider five foot two, or the horse is a lightweight Thoroughbred, and the rider over thirteen stone? Is any instruction here a lost cause? It's all very well for instructors to preach method. But what if the rider doesn't have the necessary figure to put it into practice? Yet the most unusual partnerships do exist, and successfully too. They exist because human movement has the scope to put the rider in touch with suitable receptors around the horse's body – provided the rider knows where these receptors are.

Nevertheless, this movement flexibility is a double-edged sword. It's possible to see riders with good riding figures – ones that are apparently ideally suited to the size of their horses – using their legs against the horse's ribcage like a percussionist playing the tubular bells, or steering with their arms and upper bodies as if they were riding a superbike in a race, or driving with their seats with enough power to weaken the joints of the stoutest chair.

They do so in an effort to help the horse. They do so because the brain tells us that effort brings reward, therefore *more* effort must bring more reward. They do so because, by virtue of our evolution, the brain has given us the wherewithal to prepare a meal, but also the potential to overcook it! The point is that many people learn to ride by being told to do what other people do. That's fine as long as they share the same length of leg, or arm, or body. Otherwise, it can be a very frustrating exercise. But there is another way. We can learn about the key structures of the horse's anatomy, and how they make riding possible. We can learn how these structures respond to touch and pressure. And we can learn how, by activating these structures in the right order, we can use the horse's posture to both his – and our own – advantage.

There are many attempts, in books and in magazines, to advise the would-be rider on the correct way to use his anatomy in the saddle: where his seat bones should be, at what angle; to what degree he should tilt his pelvis; and so on. But there is an almost infinite variety of human shape, and a vast number of permutations in the way these shapes impact on the horse's movements. Compared to this, there are far fewer variations in the shape of the horse.

Competitions require that we ride standard figures, or tackle standard jumps, with equal ability on both reins. But this ideal is actually at odds with the organization of the human brain because humans are usually right- or left-handed. Nevertheless, we expect it of our horses. Therefore, the only logical approach to learning to ride is not to get caught up in the minutiae of human movement but to focus on the relatively straightforward movement of the horse. This gives every rider the same chance to tap into his horse's potential, whatever shape he is.

If we look at pictures of the really great riders (great, not competitively, but, artistically) – Colonel Podhajsky of the Spanish Riding School, for example, or the Portuguese horseman Nuno Oliviera – we see them sitting quietly, their shoulders simply square with their horse's shoulders, their hips square with their horse's hips. They didn't learn to ride by throwing together some diverse ingredients of human movement and hoping it might make nouvelle cuisine. They studied the way the horse moves, and the way the horse uses his anatomy, so that they could allow their own movements to fall into line with his. Perhaps *that's* what it really means to 'think like a horse'.

Riders come in many shapes and sizes: tall, small, broad, or slim; wide hips or narrow hips; long backs, short arms, and so on. Although there might be a perceived 'ideal' figure to suit the conformation of each horse and pony – for example, one where the rider's calf lies effortlessly against the horse's lower chest, or one where the elbow, when flexed, brings the arm into perfect alignment with the bit – very rarely do these team up in real life.

Yet the short rider on the tall horse and the tall rider on the short horse may form most successful partnerships.

One type of horse may be ridden by any number of differently shaped riders, and in any number of different styles. Does this mean that most of them are wrong? Or does it mean that there is an underlying source of integrity in how the horse should be ridden, but a variety of means by which we can tap into that source.

These riders are separated by more than two thousand years of history and culture. Yet there is probably not much that separates their skills as riders. Beneath the 'camouflage' of the twenty-first century, there is the same basic human being: a unique synthesis of mental and physical ingenuity capable of sending messages to the horse, even when the means by which these messages are sent are encased in leather boots and designer jods.

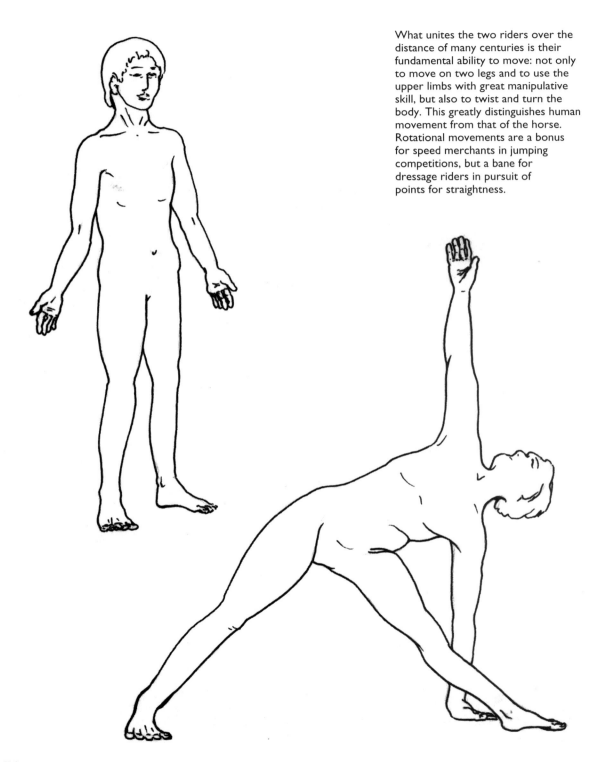

What unites the two riders over the distance of many centuries is their fundamental ability to move: not only to move on two legs and to use the upper limbs with great manipulative skill, but also to twist and turn the body. This greatly distinguishes human movement from that of the horse. Rotational movements are a bonus for speed merchants in jumping competitions, but a bane for dressage riders in pursuit of points for straightness.

Superficially, there is a certain similarity between the topline of the horse and the curves of the human spine. But we have to remember that the horse's back is not simply a human back placed horizontally. There are very significant differences.

The horse's spinal column does not have the same capacity for flexion and extension – even if he does sometimes turn himself inside out.

In contrast to humans, the horse has real flexibility and rotation only in the neck and tail.

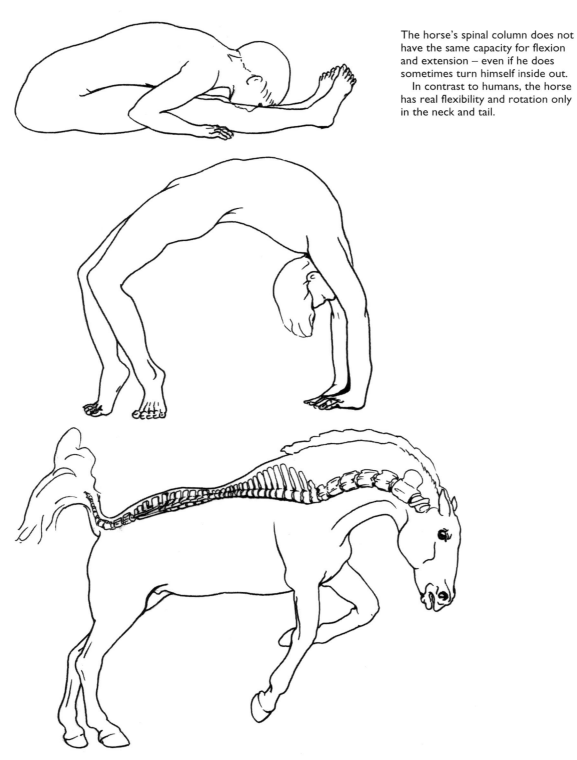

Parelli has described the horse as having six directions of movement: forwards, backwards, sideways left and right (oblique), upwards and downwards (A).

Human movements include all these, as well as the ability to twist and turn, which produces spiral movement (B).

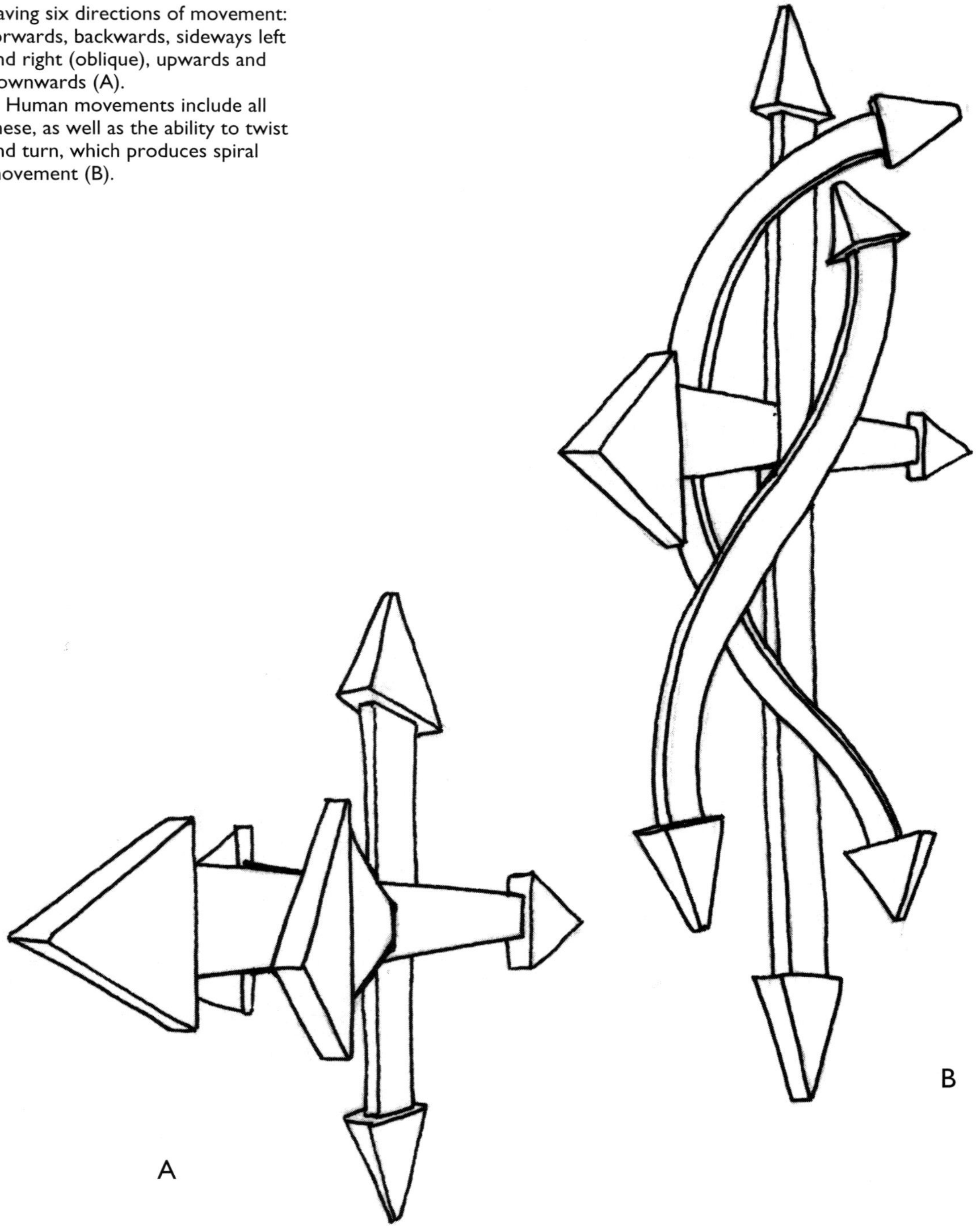

A

B

The flexibility of the human body gives the rider the scope to impose the maximum degree of sideward movement in the horse (below), or to control his horse's straightness (opposite).

The human posture is determined by many factors, not least by the proportions of the body, the degree of natural asymmetry, and the mental disposition of the individual.

Balance can be learnt, whatever our shape and size, but, like any form of training, it requires regular practice to maintain. This includes standing with equal weight on both feet, rather than resting more on one hip than the other (A), and resisting the urge to sit cross-legged (B) – in the tack room, in the office, at the dinner table, or anywhere else.

These typical poses are, like crisps and chocolate, not inherently bad for us, in small doses. But they are most unhelpful if we want to ride horses. Like junk food, they become an acceptable means of propping us up.

We cannot expect the horse to load each side of his body fifty-fifty if we sit on his back with a weight ratio of sixty-forty. If we forget to distribute our weight evenly when we're not in the saddle, we're unlikely to remember to do so when we are.

A

B

Human beings are not symmetrical. They can't be, by virtue of the distinct functions of the left and right hemispheres of the brain (A). Nevertheless, it is possible for humans to have balance without symmetry (B), but their interpretation of balance is bound to be different from that of horses.

The organization of the equine brain is different, and it is debatable whether the horse's 'natural bend' is inborn or instilled. Therefore, the relationship between symmetry and balance is one of the enduring problems of riding. It's literally a matter of – balance.

A

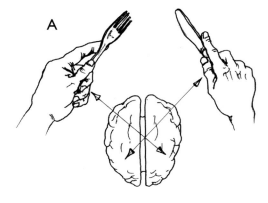

B

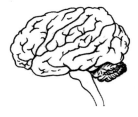

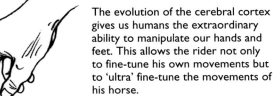

The evolution of the cerebral cortex gives us humans the extraordinary ability to manipulate our hands and feet. This allows the rider not only to fine-tune his own movements but to 'ultra' fine-tune the movements of his horse.

However, the same hands and feet can be the focal points for tension, tension which can arise anywhere in the body – for example, in the shoulders, neck, back, or simply in the breathing. This does not necessarily produce just stiffness. Tension can also result in over-manipulation.

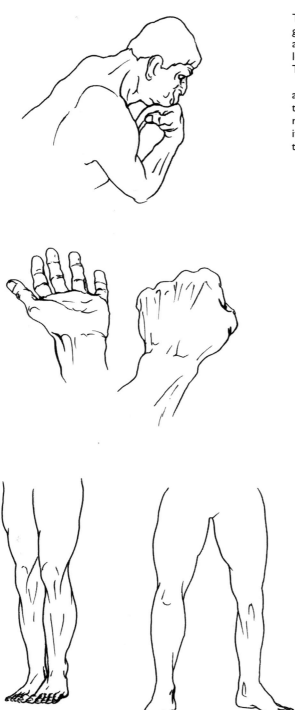

The human being is a thinking creature, capable of generating ideas. Human hands have the capacity to vie and to release, but also to grasp and to grab. Human legs allow us to stand to attention, or to stand easy. The human body can either sit up or slouch.

Successful riding depends on all these factors, the ability to give and take with the reins, to grip with the thigh or press with the heel, to brace the back and to relax it. It depends on our ability to solve problems. But it's a matter of degree. Balanced riding means finding the right balance between all these human attributes.

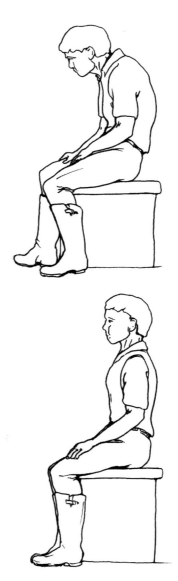

The unique combination of human faculties enables the rider to communicate his ideas to the horse. He does so using movements that are triggered by nerves, originating in the spinal cord. The horse responds to these ideas, also using nerve pathways in the spinal cord. He translates the communications of the rider into movement.

The question is, how?

3 Making the Right Connections: the Equipment───────

I was aware of the excellent effects of the spur; but I abstained from developing my principles, being prevented by an expression of one of my friends. 'It is extraordinary! It is wonderful!' he exclaimed, 'but it is a razor in the hands of a monkey.'

François Baucher, *New Method of Horsemanship*, 1842

This anecdote, written by Baucher in the early nineteenth century, may seem a touch melodramatic. But it was, after all, the Age of Romanticism, and the spirit of the age found its way into every walk of French life, including horse riding. It was characteristic of the era that the whole country – nobility, cavalry officers, writers, philosophers and poets, alike – should be gripped by an intense debate over a new method of horsemanship.

On the one hand, there was the aristocrat, Count d'Aure, who advocated the free, natural, way of riding, along the lines of hacking, hunting, and point-to-point racing, which was practised in England. On the other hand, there was François Baucher, from humble beginnings, who caught the public's imagination when he began to demonstrate lightness and balance in dressage – in a circus. He showed that by using a series of methodical suppling exercises, and by understanding the exact reciprocal action of the bit and spur, it was possible to teach the most difficult horses to go without tension or force. What is more, this could be achieved in a remarkably short space of time.

Baucher's system was not quite as new as he claimed; other charismatic horsemen had preceded him, and their horses had been trained to equal perfection. Baucher's real contribution was to examine the input of the rider in minute detail, and to quantify the results. This made it possible for him to state categorically the purpose of each aid, the effect it should have, and the order in which each should be applied.

Baucher also had a unique insight into the role of the horse's conformation, which he gained through what was then considered the unfortunate circumstance of having to ride many different types of horses. This appreciation of anatomy, combined with his logical application of the aids, enabled him to reproduce his success in training, time after time. Such was his reputation that, today, he would undoubtedly be given his own show on prime-time television.

The key to many of Baucher's suppling exercises was the strategic use of the rider's 'tools', namely the curb bit, the whip, and the spur. This suggests that Baucher's system was one of domination and reprimand. Far from it, his supreme philosophy was that these tools should always be used with prudence and tact. For example, in his *New Method of Horsemanship*, he explains:

Professors of equitation … have said that the spurs are to punish the horse. [They] exclaim, you attack with the spur, horses that are sensitive, … full of fire and action, horses whose powerful make leads them to become unmanageable, in spite of the hardest bits and the most vigorous arms! Yes, and it is with the spur that I will moderate the fury of these too fiery animals … It is with the spur, aided of course by the hand, that I will make the most stubborn natures kind.

To 'moderate the fury' by using the spur: that does indeed take tact. Today, the bit and the spur are not the only tools for consideration in the rider's instrumentarium. I wonder what Baucher would have made of the vast selection of equipment on offer in our mail-order catalogues? The choice is immense, from reins to martingales, from whips to boots, right down to something as fundamental as the saddle and bridle. These are today's means by which the rider communicates the aids to his horse.

It is important to realize that each piece of equipment is not only an interface but a connector. It connects one part of the rider's body with a part of the horse, as well as occupying the space between them. It depends on the choice of equipment, and its application, as to whether it makes a good connection or a poor connection: whether the horse can hear the rider clearly and uninterruptedly, or only intermittently, through a background of hisses and crackles.

It could be argued that the effect of the rider's equipment should be neglible, in the sense that it is only 'a poor workman who blames his tools'. Indeed, I knew a man who always rode his horses in the same type of bit and with his own, favourite saddle. Yet, such was his sensitivity towards the specific needs of each horse that it never crossed his mind to try anything else. Higher up the scale, there is a wonderful photograph of the famous horseman, Nuno Oliviera, riding Corsario at the *passage* with only a string to the horse's mouth. And then there is a whole volume of photographs of Pat Parelli riding his horses with no equipment at all. These are, of course, exceptional horsemen. But for most of us, the equipment – like the saddle, bridle, bit, spurs,

whip, and, incidentally, the horse's shoes will always be an integral part of the transmission process between horse and rider.

The saddle, bridle, and so on, are the first things to make contact with the horse's skin, not the rider himself. For this reason, each piece of equipment has an impact on part of the horse's sensorium: namely, on his sense of touch. It is therefore necessary to consider the effect of our equipment on the horse before we can understand how to put it into operation.

As human beings, we are used to wearing clothes. We get accustomed to this almost as soon as we are born, and we quickly learn to tolerate belts around the waist, collars round the neck, shoes on the feet, gloves on the hands, and glasses across the bridge of the nose. These are areas of the body with high levels of touch sensitivity, either because they are potentially vulnerable or because they were (originally) required to relay information about the environment.

Pressure receptors under the skin learn to differentiate between touch that is going to be acceptable, and touch that might be uncomfortable. In humans, they are given a lot of time to adapt. The horse's pressure receptors do not have the benefit of the same gradual process of education. Of course, we allow the horse time (weeks or months) to grow accustomed to wearing the bridle or the saddle. But what is this compared to the years of acclimatization that the human skin undergoes? Yet, the horse, very quickly, has to learn to tolerate the pressure of foreign materials in intimate contact with his body, and in areas where instinct tells him he is at the most risk: round the head, over the poll, on the back, and in the mouth!

Perhaps we do not always realize just how much we ask of the horse when we add yet another pad under the saddle, or decide – because our horse went badly in last week's lesson – to exchange one type of bit for another. In his book *Academic Equitation* (published originally in 1949), General Decarpentry devotes a whole chapter not to saddles and saddle-fitting, but to bits and the horse's mouth (chapter four, The Mouthpiece). He describes in detail how mouths can be differently shaped, and that such differences can affect various parts of the mouth, from the width of the bars, the conformation of the jaw, the 'split' of the mouth, the position of the teeth, including the tushes, to the fleshiness of the lips and the thickness of the tongue. Any rider, reading these words, who knows the dimensions of all these structures within the first six inches of his horse's oral cavity should award himself ten-out-of-ten and go to the top of the class.

It is alarming to think that, for most people, fitting a bit means roughly estimating the overall width of the horse's mouth: rarely do they ever look *inside* it. There are hundreds of bits on the market. How does anybody choose? Perhaps, one day somebody will invent a user-friendly 'oral profiler' in the same way that we now have width gauges for saddles. Tongue evasions might then become a thing of the past.

In saddle-fitting, however, things have – fortunately – moved on. Today, it is within every rider's capability to check the width of their saddle, and for a good reason. If there is one piece of equipment that embodies the sum total of the horse's most primeval fears, it must be the saddle. The vice-like grip of the tree, combined with the shifting weight of the rider, is the predator epitomized. Saddle design has improved greatly in recent years, and, thanks to increasing rider awareness, most horses no longer have to suffer years of excruciating back pain.

But there are still subtle problems caused by improper balance. These can be more than a little responsible for interrupting the horse's ability to move as a unified whole. For example, under the front of the arch, there can be pressure on the multi-layered intersection of muscles that feed under the scapula. Under the rear of the saddle, there can be pressure on the thoracolumbar fascia. Under the middle of the saddle, there can be – well, just pressure. Rocking of the saddle is one of the easiest problems to identify; it's also one of the hardest to put right.

And then there are the horseshoes. It has to be said that humans have a logic that is probably a source of great bewilderment to the rest of the animal kingdom. With the best intentions of getting the horse gently accustomed to the saddle and bridle, we put them on and then promptly whisk them away, long before the pressure sensors have had time to acclimatize. What do we do with shoes? One day, we suddenly have them attached to the horse's feet – and then we leave them there for six to eight weeks. Would we, ourselves, put up with wearing the same footwear, day in, day out, without relief, even when we go to bed?

Yet what could have a more profound effect on the horse's movement than attaching pieces of metal to his feet? It's not just a matter of weight. It's the whole question of balance: the width of the shoe, the length of the shoe, the placing of the shoe in relation to the conformation of the limb, the placing of all four shoes in relation to the conformation of the horse.

Shoes can be the most helpful piece of equipment to the rider; they can be the most damaging to the horse. Good shoeing can help the rider along on his quest for lightness. Poor shoeing can prevent the horse from ever getting his own feet off the ground. Balanced shoeing is not just the one that improves the arc of flight of the front foot. Truly balanced shoeing brings the hind feet under the horse's body, so that he can lift his back and swing with his front legs without risk of interference from his own toes.

Without the correct interpretation of movement by the farrier through shoeing, the horse cannot use any of the vital structures of his topline to support the rider: namely, the long back muscles and the fascia. Then every piece of equipment, the saddle, the girth, the spur, the bit, becomes a blockade. It impinges – because the circle of motion, which passes over the back and under the belly, has been broken – broken by an imbalance in the feet.

It is not possible, in the space of one chapter of one book, to highlight all the pros and cons of equipment that, elsewhere, has been the subject of an entire book, or books. It is possible only to illustrate trends in our modern equipment and place them in the context of the horse's anatomy. Despite thousands of years of horsemanship, the equipment we use is still largely an ongoing experiment – if not in form, then in the choice of modern materials. Whether riding represents to us a competitive or an artistic endeavour, the one thing we don't want is to be defeated by our own 'tools'.

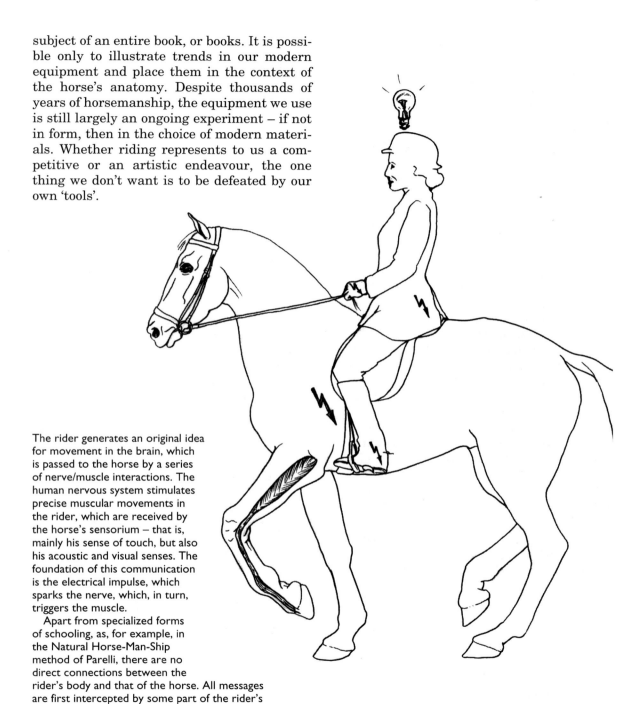

The rider generates an original idea for movement in the brain, which is passed to the horse by a series of nerve/muscle interactions. The human nervous system stimulates precise muscular movements in the rider, which are received by the horse's sensorium – that is, mainly his sense of touch, but also his acoustic and visual senses. The foundation of this communication is the electrical impulse, which sparks the nerve, which, in turn, triggers the muscle.

Apart from specialized forms of schooling, as, for example, in the Natural Horse-Man-Ship method of Parelli, there are no direct connections between the rider's body and that of the horse. All messages are first intercepted by some part of the rider's equipment, be it saddle, bridle, reins, bit, boots, or spurs. The choice of equipment, therefore, has a tremendous impact on riding – above all, on the horse's ability to read our minds!

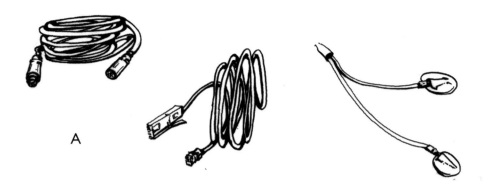

A

The successful implementation of movement depends on two things: one is the ability to coordinate the moving parts, the other is the ability to guide them, without harm, through the environment. The nervous system, in its many guises, is responsible for all this.

The function of the nervous system is to relay information, not only to and from muscles, but to and from tendons, ligaments, joint capsules, and, most importantly, the skin. Just as technology has given us a variety of leads through which some form of electrical impulse can be conveyed (A), so the nervous system comprises different 'leads' to serve a similar purpose.

Part of the function of the nervous system is to keep the brain updated with information that might influence the possible choice of movement: for example, the need for evasive action. This information is provided by sensors that measure the effect of pressure, weight, heat or cold (B) on the skin and subcutaneous tissues. The body pools this information with measurements from other sources, such as joint capsules, to determine balance.

At the deeper level, the 'wiring' of the nerves relays at least three types of information:

• The current state of play in a certain type of tissue (such as the degree of relaxation or spasm in a muscle, or the tension across a joint).
• The potential for a state of alarm (for example, to avoid injury).
• The instruction to change the current state (for example, to produce a muscle contraction).

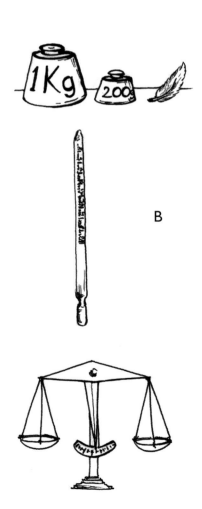

B

C

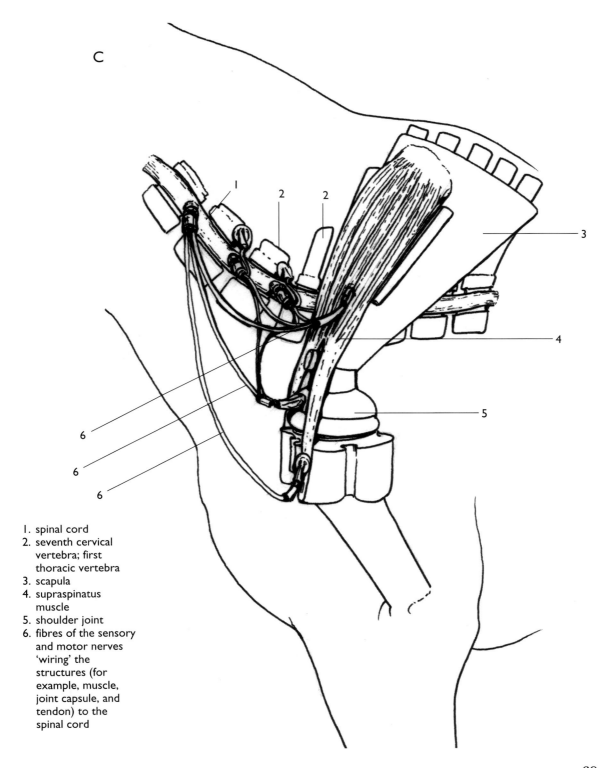

1. spinal cord
2. seventh cervical
   vertebra; first
   thoracic vertebra
3. scapula
4. supraspinatus
   muscle
5. shoulder joint
6. fibres of the sensory
   and motor nerves
   'wiring' the
   structures (for
   example, muscle,
   joint capsule, and
   tendon) to the
   spinal cord

When you think about it, the rider occupies only a very small area of the horse's body (B, D). The bulk of effective musculature is either fore or aft (A, C). The rider is utterly dependent on his equipment to make the right connection between, for example, his leg and the horse's side, or his hand and the horse's mouth. Without the right connections, the aids become distorted or meaningless.

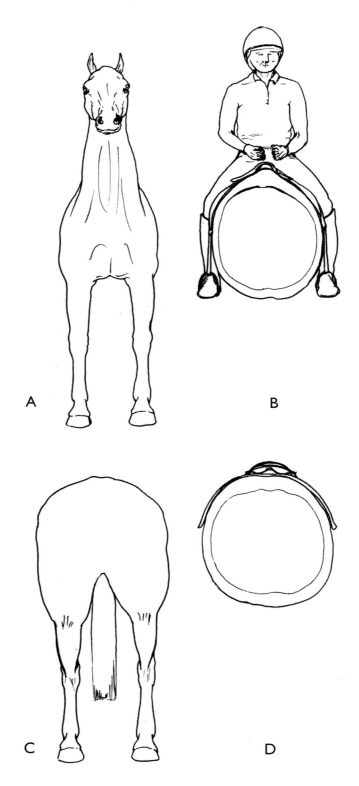

A

B

C

D

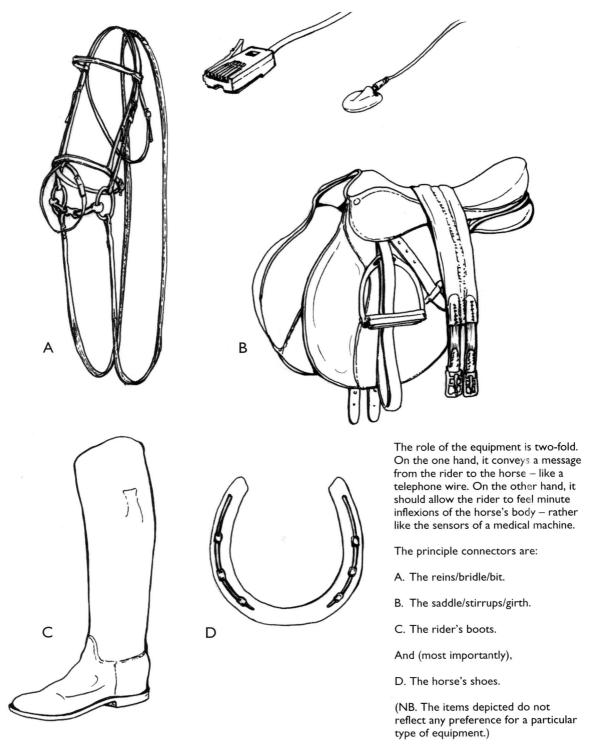

The role of the equipment is two-fold. On the one hand, it conveys a message from the rider to the horse – like a telephone wire. On the other hand, it should allow the rider to feel minute inflexions of the horse's body – rather like the sensors of a medical machine.

The principle connectors are:

A. The reins/bridle/bit.

B. The saddle/stirrups/girth.

C. The rider's boots.

And (most importantly),

D. The horse's shoes.

(NB. The items depicted do not reflect any preference for a particular type of equipment.)

Connecting the hand to the mouth.

The reins are a direct extension of the rider's hands, and the bit is the means by which the messages from the hands are conveyed to the jaw.

The head, which comprises the bony skull (and brain), musculature, and probably the most dense network of nerve fibres anywhere in the body, is the direct recipient of all the gestures that we, as riders, make with our hands, arms and upper bodies. (A)

The bit is used to send messages from the rider, to relay sensory information back to the rider, or simply for a game of tug-of-war!

Most of the sensory, and sensitive, nerve fibres are carried in the massive trigeminus nerve, which branches into the infraorbitalis and mandibularis nerves. Most of the motor fibres are part of the facialis nerve (which originates in the interimediofacialis nerve).

All these nerves stem from an area close to the base of the skull (B). Any pinching or constriction, either by the bridle, or by the effect of the rider's hand, is bound to be the source of a major headache to the horse.

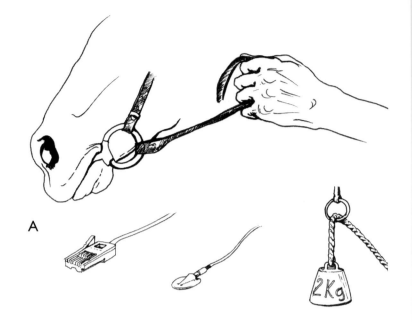

A

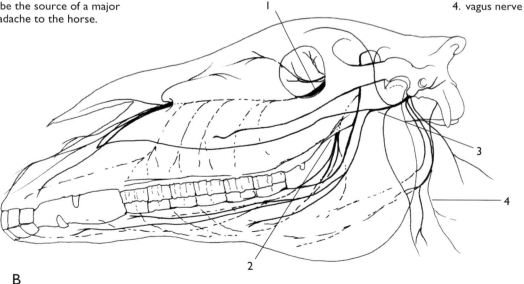

1. maxillaris nerve
2. mandibularis nerve
3. facialis nerve
4. vagus nerve

B

72

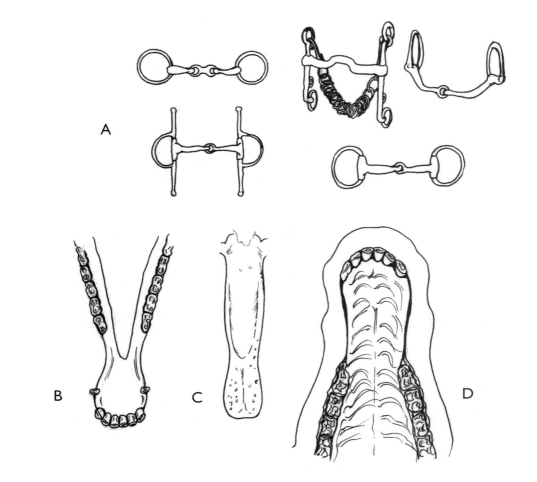

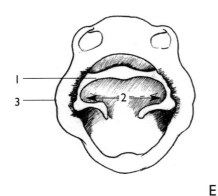

Whichever type of bit we choose (A), we have to take into consideration: B, the width and calibre of the lower jaw, and the position of the teeth, including the space between the tushes and the premolars. (Note that in mares, with no visible tushes, this area of the gum can still be particularly sensitive.); C, the width and thickness of the tongue; D, the arch of the palate.

For the purposes of fitting the bit, we should take into consideration E (which shows a cross-section of the mouth): (1) the clearance of the palate; (2) the spread of the tongue; and (3) the 'fleshiness' of the lips.

The lips are manipulated by motor nerves, which serve muscles such as the orbicularis oris muscle and the levator nasolabialis muscle (not shown). The tongue, itself, is a muscular structure, and is manipulated by a series of muscles that insert around its base. In addition to this, the entire oral cavity (the cheeks, the palate, the lips and the tongue), are endowed with a high concentration of sensory nerve endings.

73

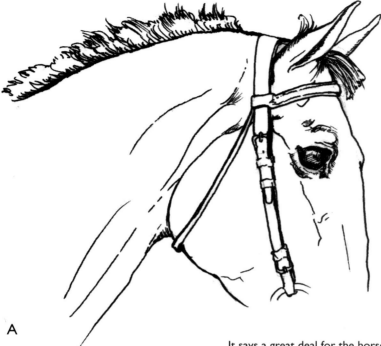

A

It says a great deal for the horse's level of tolerance that he is able to wear a mesh of straps around his head, some of which are directly attached to a piece of metal through the mouth.

The fit of the headpiece of the bridle (A) or training halter is just as influential as the position of the bit, for the following reasons:

The skull and jaw bone (B) have three places of insertion for the long neck muscles: (1) occipital protuberance (top of the skull), (2) mastoid process (just below the ear), and (3) sternomandibular process (on the bottom jaw bone). (Strictly speaking, the occiput is an indirect place of insertion for muscles since they attach first to the nuchal ligament, which then attaches to the skull.)

Compared to other bony areas of muscle origin and insertion, these places are very small (only a couple of centimetres across). The power of high-calibre muscles, such as the splenius muscle (4), the brachiocephalic muscle (5), or the sternomandibularis muscle (6), is concentrated on an extremely small area of bone. Yet the bridle rests against what amounts to very important intersections between the neck and head. In particular, the browband and throatlash can press against a small but significant muscle which manipulates the ear, the parotidoauricularis muscle (7).

If, for any reason, the horse finds it necessary to evade the bit, he can try to get his tongue over the bit, he can set or cross his jaw, or he can retract the tongue. Whatever he tries, he must tense the muscles around the jaw to do it, which probably only makes him uncomfortable somewhere else.

Certainly, if he draws the tongue back, he tenses the long throat muscles (8), which extend as far as the sternum, and effectively blocks the action of all the other neck muscles as far as the shoulders (C).

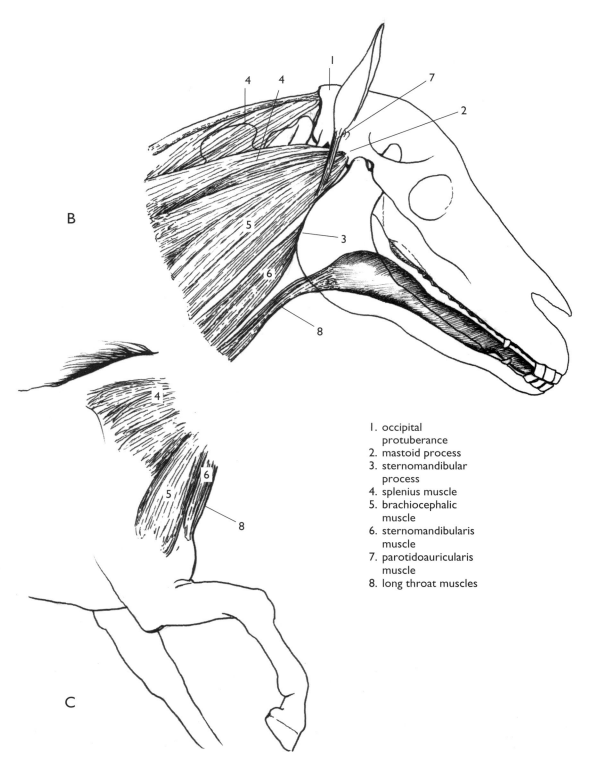

B

C

1. occipital
   protuberance
2. mastoid process
3. sternomandibular
   process
4. splenius muscle
5. brachiocephalic
   muscle
6. sternomandibularis
   muscle
7. parotidoauricularis
   muscle
8. long throat muscles

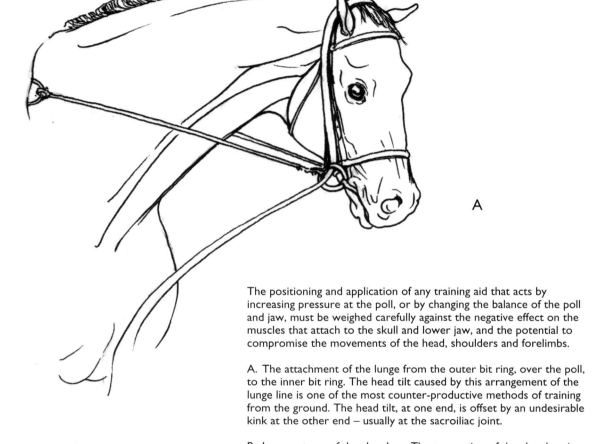

A

The positioning and application of any training aid that acts by increasing pressure at the poll, or by changing the balance of the poll and jaw, must be weighed carefully against the negative effect on the muscles that attach to the skull and lower jaw, and the potential to compromise the movements of the head, shoulders and forelimbs.

A. The attachment of the lunge from the outer bit ring, over the poll, to the inner bit ring. The head tilt caused by this arrangement of the lunge line is one of the most counter-productive methods of training from the ground. The head tilt, at one end, is offset by an undesirable kink at the other end – usually at the sacroiliac joint.

B. Incorrect use of the chambon. The true action of the chambon is to raise the bit in the mouth when the head is raised above a certain position. This is because the chambon headpiece is fixed to the headpiece of the bridle, and doesn't move independently. But it is only really effective if the horse generates enough impulsion with the hind legs. This requires (a) the horse to be shod with sufficient length on the hind feet, to encourage such a stride, and (b) the trainer to maintain the forwards momentum with the support of the lunge whip. Without adequate drive, the horse can brace himself against the chambon. He simply runs along the ground, probably with a headache.

C. The rope halter. Control of the horse by pressure halter is currently in vogue. People quickly resort to it when the horse is being 'difficult'. However, often the horse's behaviour is caused by a physical problem, such as a sore sacroiliac joint. In such cases there is already tension at the poll, if not pain. Correct use of this equipment requires accurate timing and sensitivity. Otherwise it is the cause of untold harm.

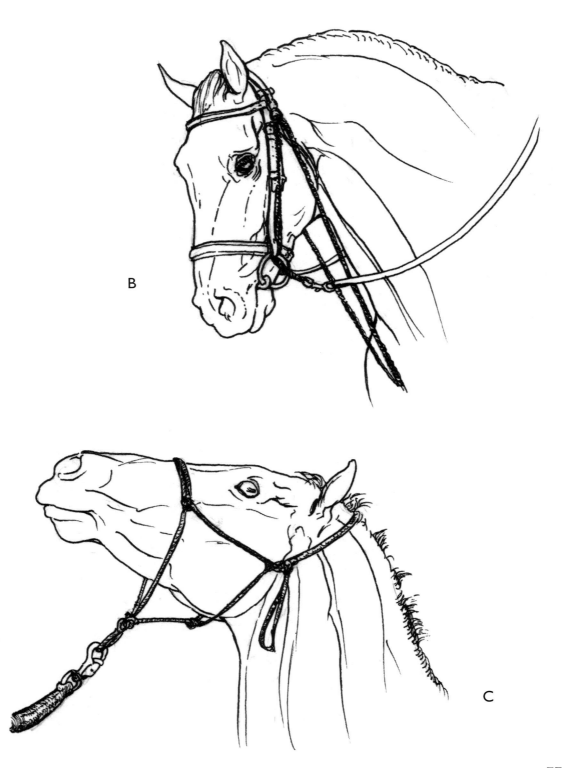

The fit, design, and pressure distribution of the saddle has far-reaching consequences for the entire muscle system of the horse's body.

1. longissimus muscle
2. gluteus medius muscle
3. iliocostalis muscle
4. external oblique abdominal muscle
5. intercostal muscles
6. serratus ventralis muscle
7. caudal serratus dorsalis muscle
8. cervical portion of longissimus muscle
9. spinalis muscle (wither polster)

10. splenius muscle
11 and 12. longissimus atlantis and capitis muscles
13. semispinalis muscle (insertion at the poll)
14. scapula
15. deltoid muscle, overlying the infraspinatus muscle
16. triceps muscle
17. common and lateral digital extensor muscles and tendons
18. first rib
19. superficial and deep pectoral muscles

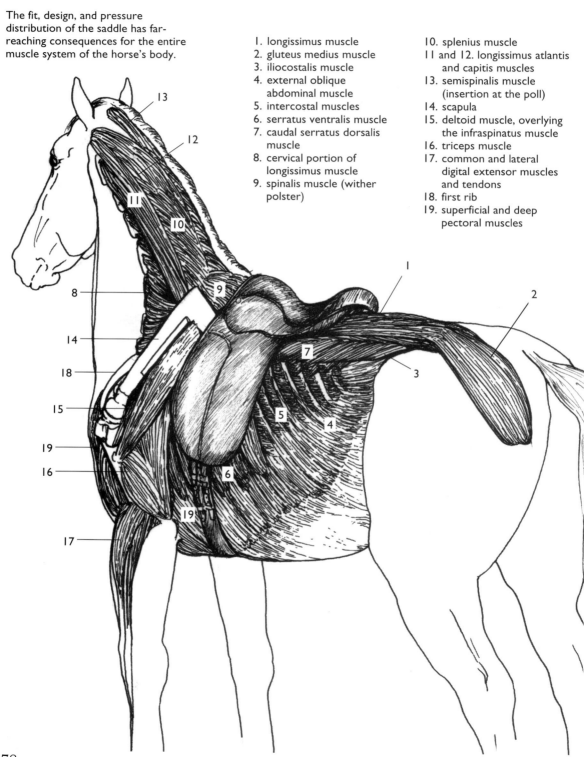

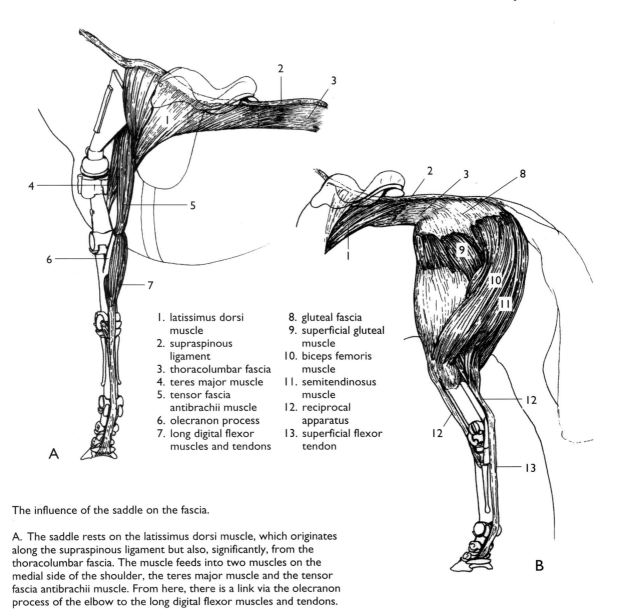

1. latissimus dorsi muscle
2. supraspinous ligament
3. thoracolumbar fascia
4. teres major muscle
5. tensor fascia antibrachii muscle
6. olecranon process
7. long digital flexor muscles and tendons
8. gluteal fascia
9. superficial gluteal muscle
10. biceps femoris muscle
11. semitendinosus muscle
12. reciprocal apparatus
13. superficial flexor tendon

The influence of the saddle on the fascia.

A. The saddle rests on the latissimus dorsi muscle, which originates along the supraspinous ligament but also, significantly, from the thoracolumbar fascia. The muscle feeds into two muscles on the medial side of the shoulder, the teres major muscle and the tensor fascia antibrachii muscle. From here, there is a link via the olecranon process of the elbow to the long digital flexor muscles and tendons.

B. The thoracolumbar fascia extends back over the hindquarters, where it is called the gluteal fascia, a principle tissue of origin for the superficial gluteal muscle, the biceps femoris muscle, and the semitendinosus muscle. These muscles insert on fascia that surrounds the stifle joint. This fascia connects to the ligaments of the patella and serves as an intermediary link to the reciprocal apparatus as well as the muscles and tendons of the lower hind leg.

The fascia is the 'harness' of the body's locomotor system. The muscles pull and the skeleton follows, but, if it were not for the fascia and associated connective tissue structures, such as tendons and ligaments, the power would remain disconnected from the frame. If the fascia (in this case, the thoracolumbar fascia) becomes trapped by an ill-fitting, or badly balanced saddle, it will have the same effect as traces that snag on the driving shaft: it can truly upset the applecart.

79

1. saddle
2. ribs
3. sternum
4. vertebra
5. pectoral muscle
6. latissimus dorsi and serratus ventralis muscles
7. longissimus and iliocostalis muscles
8. multifidi muscle system

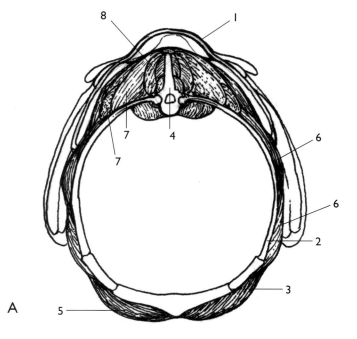

A

Three cross-sections through the horse's chest and saddle:

A. Rear withers and front arch of the saddle.

B. Mid-thoracic region and waist of the saddle.

C. Rear thoracic region towards the cantle area of the saddle.

Beneath the thoracolumbar fascia and latissimus dorsi muscle are a multitude of smaller muscles, which extend from the quarters, along the rump, pass under the shoulder blades, and insert on the base of the neck. Although the longissimus and iliocostalis muscles are long, they insert segmentally, at regular intervals along the spine and heads of the ribs. All other muscles span short segments but form a continuous system along the whole spine.

The three subdivisions of the saddle affect the way in which different portions of the back musculature performs. They can allow an integrated movement, or they can isolate portions of the muscles and create artificial separations.

All these muscles are both bound and separated by fascial layers. It is these layers, made of strong connective tissue, that define the shape of the back. Remember, the muscle tissue is elastic, but the fascial tissue is plastic.

Any part of the saddle – a narrow arch, a badly angled stirrup bar, a hard lump of flocking – has the potential to 'pin down' the fascia, and prevent the muscles from working fluently. Above all, the width of the arch is crucial, to accommodate the shoulder blades. This presents a problem in saddle-fitting if the horse has wide shoulders but is hollow behind the withers (D), or if the horse is broad round the waist but narrow across the shoulders (E).

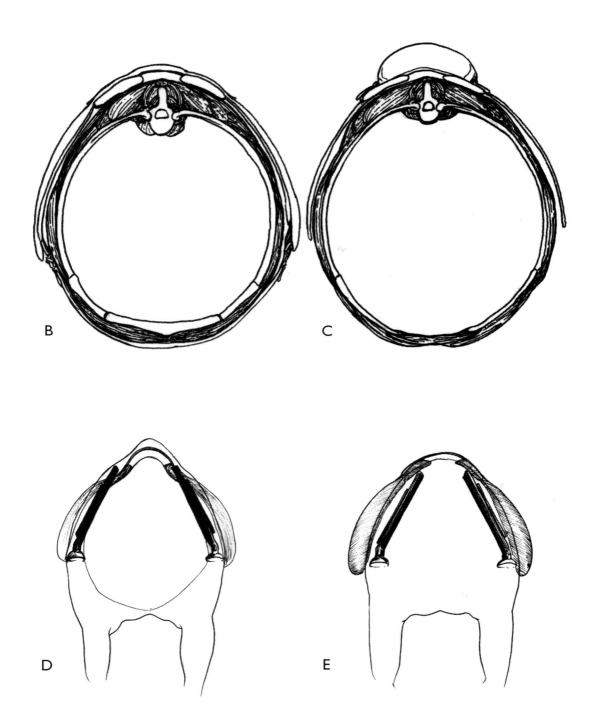

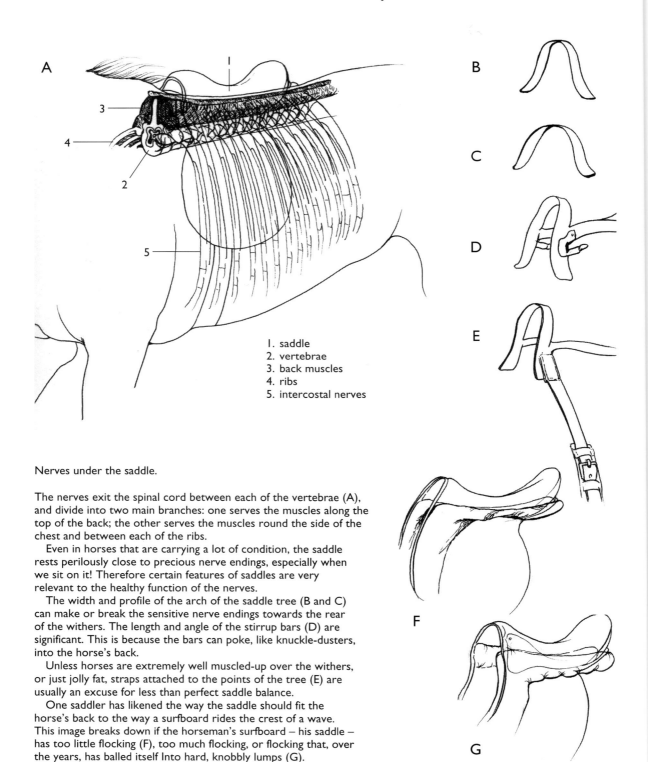

A

B

C

D

E

F

G

3

4

2

5

I

1. saddle
2. vertebrae
3. back muscles
4. ribs
5. intercostal nerves

Nerves under the saddle.

The nerves exit the spinal cord between each of the vertebrae (A), and divide into two main branches: one serves the muscles along the top of the back; the other serves the muscles round the side of the chest and between each of the ribs.

Even in horses that are carrying a lot of condition, the saddle rests perilously close to precious nerve endings, especially when we sit on it! Therefore certain features of saddles are very relevant to the healthy function of the nerves.

The width and profile of the arch of the saddle tree (B and C) can make or break the sensitive nerve endings towards the rear of the withers. The length and angle of the stirrup bars (D) are significant. This is because the bars can poke, like knuckle-dusters, into the horse's back.

Unless horses are extremely well muscled-up over the withers, or just jolly fat, straps attached to the points of the tree (E) are usually an excuse for less than perfect saddle balance.

One saddler has likened the way the saddle should fit the horse's back to the way a surfboard rides the crest of a wave. This image breaks down if the horseman's surfboard – his saddle – has too little flocking (F), too much flocking, or flocking that, over the years, has balled itself Into hard, knobbly lumps (G).

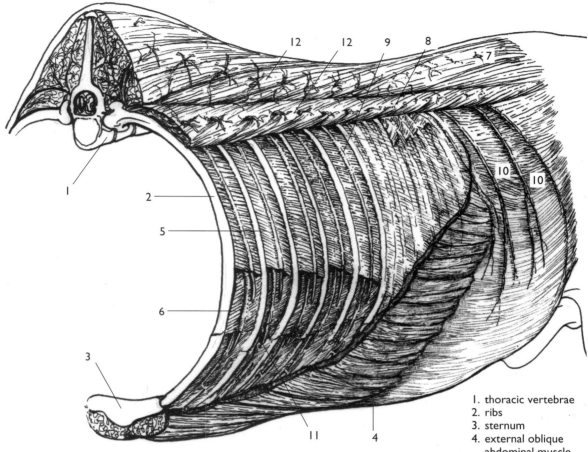

1. thoracic vertebrae
2. ribs
3. sternum
4. external oblique abdominal muscle
5. external intercostal muscle
6. internal intercostal muscle
7. longissimus muscle
8. iliocostalis muscle
9. superficial branch of intercostal nerve
10. ventral branches of the lumbar nerves
11. deep branch of the intercostal nerves
12. dorsal branches of nerves to the back muscles

The arrangement of nerves along the horse's back and between the ribs is of vital importance to the art of riding. The nerves are arranged segmentally, and we can think of each segment of the back muscles as having a corresponding intercostal space.

In this diagram, the layers of muscles surrounding the ribcage are cut away to reveal the long strands of nerves that innervate the intercostal muscles. The corresponding branches of the same nerve roots are shown radiating through the long back muscles.

We have to bear in mind that both the saddle and the rider's leg come into close contact with these nerves. The purpose of the leg aid is to stimulate a reflex action along the nerve pathways by applying pressure at strategic points along the muscles. Pressure has the effect of changing the tone of the muscle (or part of it), and the body is 'fooled' into responding with a postural change. For example, pressure on the lower third of the intercostal space between the twelfth and thirteenth rib causes the corresponding part of the back to flinch. When pressure is applied on both sides of the horse at the same time, the bilateral 'flinch' results in the back muscles lifting and, therefore, bracing the spine. The horse's back, literally, comes up under the rider, giving him a well-sprung seat to sit on, rather than a saggy sofa.

The reciprocal response between the sides of the horse and his back muscles can be activated at any point along the ribcage and abdomen using the rider's calf or heel. But the exact location along the nerve at which the aid is applied – whether at the nerve ending or in the middle of its length – depends on the rider's style, his intention and his choice of leg wear.

 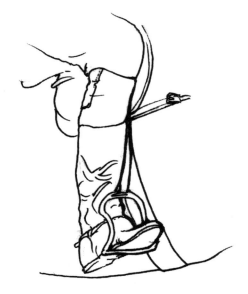

(*Above*) The rider's legs are the only part of the human anatomy to be in constant contact with the horse's body (unless we are riding bare back).

The choice of boot, its texture and stiffness, will have a significant effect on the way the leg aid is applied. The rider has to decide in what measure he requires precision, flexibility, or just plain old comfort (not shown!). The design of the riding boot, or half chap, also determines where the rider can apply the leg aid. The lower down the ribcage (towards the pectoral or abdominal muscles) the leg aid is applied, the more the emphasis will be on lift of the whole torso of the horse, rather than on simply propelling him forwards.

(*Right*) The layers of intercostal muscles are cut away to reveal the parallel arrangement of the nerves. (The upper half of the structures shown are covered by the latissimus dorsi and serratus ventalis muscles, which are not shown here.)

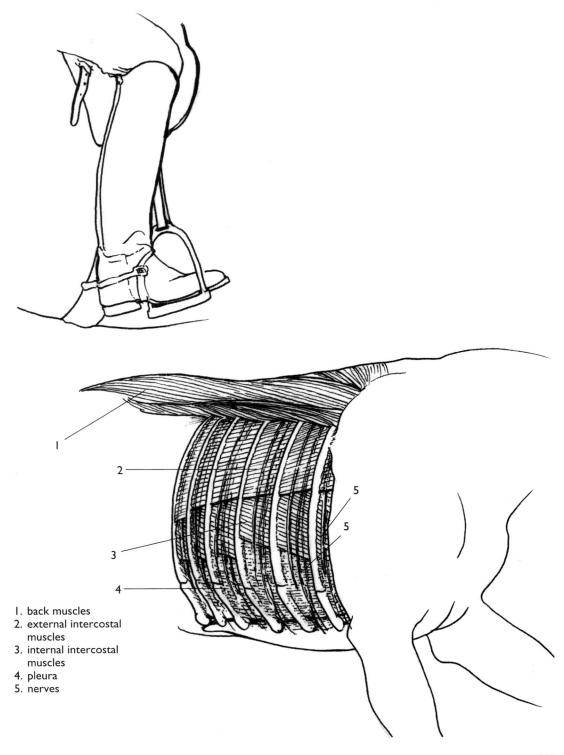

1. back muscles
2. external intercostal
   muscles
3. internal intercostal
   muscles
4. pleura
5. nerves

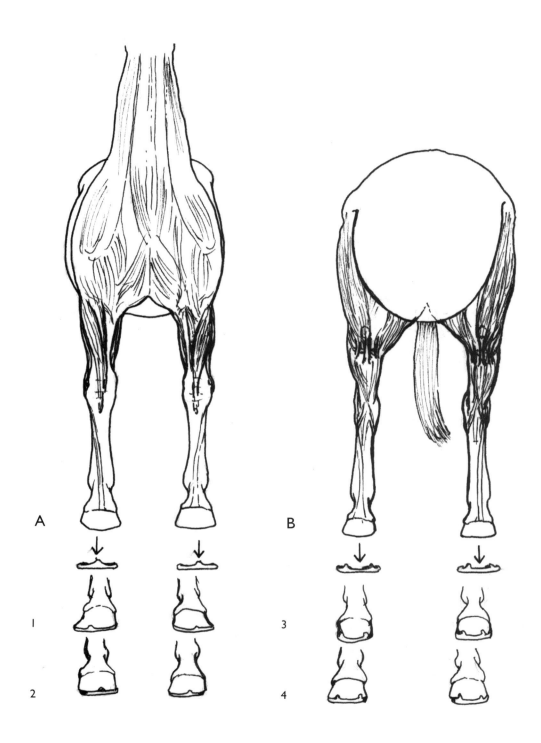

A

B

1

2

3

4

Foot balance.

For the majority of riders, the shod horse is the norm. This means that shoeing is a vital part of the rider's equipment. The horseshoe is to the rider what the tyre is to the rally driver. It can make the difference not only between grip or slip but between a sound suspension unit and a broken one. Good shoeing is the difference between mechanical superlatives and a mechanical disaster.

Originally, horseshoes served the purpose of protecting the hoof wall from breaking up when the horse was travelling long distances over stony ground. However, the presence of the horseshoe also changes the flight pattern of the limb and determines the way in which the foot lands on the ground. When the demands of riding begin to exceed those of simply moving from A to B, the support, or interference, of the shoe becomes significant. The shoe becomes an integral part of the horse's biomechanics, not just a piece of metal tacked onto the end of the foot.

On the medial (inner) side of the limb, the shoe supports not only the horse's leg but also the bulk of the horse's body weight. On the lateral (outer) side, the shoe supports the outer edges of the joints.

In the forelimb (A), the suspension of the chest, provided by the pectoral muscles, bears down on the inside edge of the shoe. However, the muscles that produce the swing of the forelimb are located on the outside of the limb. There is no case for having more width of shoe under the horse's body while skimping on the support for the lateral edge of the hoof – especially as the joints of the forelimb have only lateral and medial ligaments to hold them in alignment. If the medial wall of the foot is too high, or the foot is left with flares (1), the collateral joint ligaments will be strained when the limb moves through the stance phase of a stride and is forced down by the weight of the horse's body.

In the hind limb (B), the powerful muscles are located on the outside of the quarters and thigh, but the large structures of the stifle and hock are on the inside of the limb, underneath the horse's body. Again, there is no case for leaving these medial structures, and their ligaments, without support from the bearing surface of the horseshoe, either by wedging the foot into a shoe that is too tight, or by shortening the shoe's medial branch.

It is perhaps worth considering that although the shoes are positioned so that they balance the limbs equally when the horse is not being ridden, with the rider on board the horse effectively becomes wider (C). This places even more responsibility on the outer rim of the shoe if the lateral ligaments of the leg, especially those of the fetlock and pastern, are not to suffer strain.

In figure A, poor foot balance in the front feet is caused by: (1) flares; (2) inadequate lateral support of the shoe. In B, poor foot balance in the hind feet is caused by: (3) hooves 'cramped' into shoes that are too small; (4) inadequate medial support of the shoe.

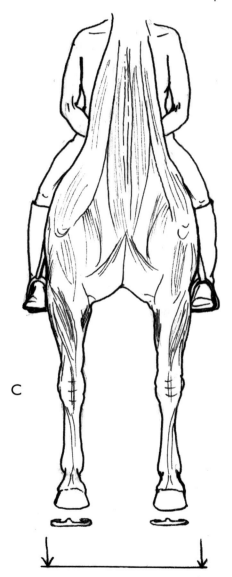

C

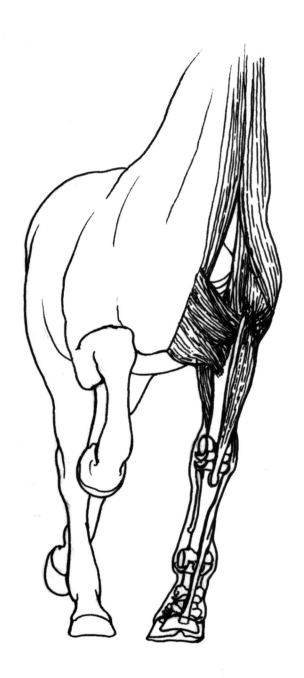

A

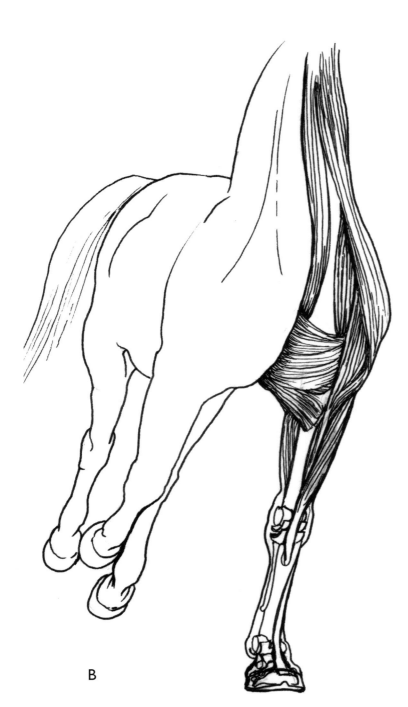

B

The importance of foot balance in movement.

The moment the foot is shod, the way in which the hoof lands becomes predetermined. The horse can no longer use the natural cutting edge of the hoof rim to sink into the ground and absorb the weight of the body. The natural expansion of the hoof wall is also restricted.

If the foot is shod in such a way that the weight of the horse bears down through the outer (lateral) edge of the joints, the limb is significantly out of balance. From the shoulder joint down to the fetlock, pastern and coffin joints, the alignment of the limb is controlled only by the presence of ligaments. To a certain extent, these ligaments are forgiving, but they cannot protect the joints indefinitely under this sort of unnatural wear.

Imagine the consequences for the joints of the lower limb, the shoulder joint, the pectoral muscles, and the muscles at the base of the neck, if the horse has to do hours of slow trot work with the kind of foot balance shown in figure A.

At a canter, or gallop (B), a well-balanced platform for the forelimb becomes even more important during the phase when the other three limbs are off the ground.

The illustrations show a mechanical approximation of the joints' hinge-like construction. This makes it clear that the shape of the joints does not allow them to compensate for any twisting movement imposed by a badly fitted shoe.

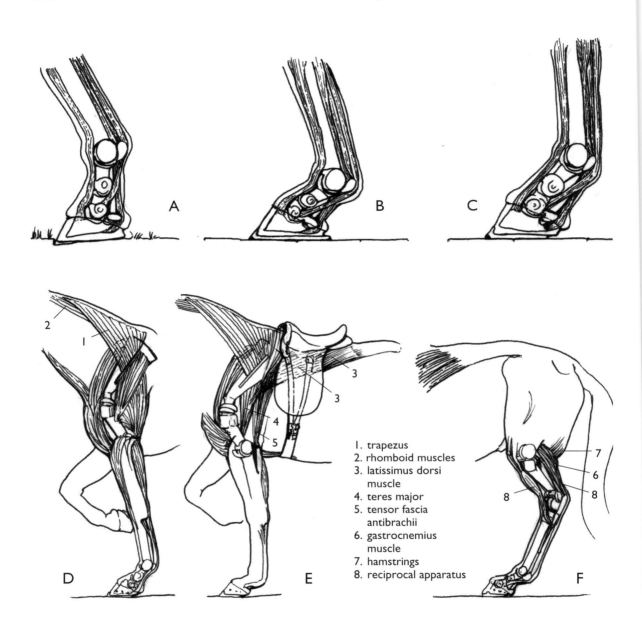

1. trapezus
2. rhomboid muscles
3. latissimus dorsi muscle
4. teres major
5. tensor fascia antibrachii
6. gastrocnemius muscle
7. hamstrings
8. reciprocal apparatus

A. On a forgiving surface, both the unshod and shod foot have ways of relieving pressure on the joints. In particular, the unshod foot can use the roll of the rim of the hoof, the natural elasticity of the hoof wall, and the expansion of the concave sole to absorb the energy of impact.

B. On a harder surface, these natural mechanisms are not available to the shod foot. The impact of the stride has to be absorbed to a greater degree through the fetlock joint and suspensory apparatus. For this reason, the 'heel' of the foot must be well supported.

C. The shoe that is too short abdicates any responsibility for supporting the limb. This puts a tremendous strain on the superficial and deep digital flexor tendons, on the suspensory apparatus, on the check ligaments, and on the muscles in the middle third of the limb.

G

D. In order to relieve pressure on the heels, including the area of the navicular bone and bursa, the horse learns to brace himself through the muscles of the chest and neck – especially through the trapezus and rhomboid muscles in front of the withers (1 and 2). In effect, he throws himself into an invisible collar.

E. The effect of inadequate shoe support is intensified if the arch of the saddle, the saddle balance, or the girthing arrangement, impinges on the action of the latissimus dorsi muscle (3). This muscle feeds into two muscles on the medial side of the shoulder – the teres major (4) and the tensor fascia antibrachii (5). When the forelimb takes the weight through the stance phase of the stride, the latissimus dorsi muscle prevents the spine from buckling upwards, and encourages the forwards momentum of the horse's body – if the saddle allows. However, the length of the stride will be steadily shortened if it's compromised by a short shoe or an ill-fitting saddle.

F. If the heels of the hind feet are unsupported, the horse braces himself through the muscles that insert towards the rear of the stifle joint – for example, the gastrocnemius muscle (6) and the hamstrings (7). This blocks the reciprocal apparatus of the hind leg (8) and prevents the horse from flexing the joints. The consequence is lack of impulsion, a stiff back, and no lift of the forehand.

G. The length of shoe is crucial to the horse's stride. In other words, if you want maximum lift, you have to have maximum support.

4 Communication Lines: the Anatomy of the Aids

Instead of having a book full of rules that govern all situations... there are only goals and principles and adjustments to fit situations.

Pat Parelli, *Natural Horse-Man-Ship*, 1993

The aids are the legs, the hands, the weight of the rider, the whip, the caress, the voice, and the use of extraneous circumstances.

General Decarpentry, *Academic Equitation*, 1949

Often one hears of an extraordinary rider simply because he has good hands. Rarely does one hear of a great horseman because be knows how to use his legs properly.

Nuno Oliveira, *Reflections on Equestrian Art*, 1976

The real *rassembler* [collection] consists in collecting the forces of the horse in his centre in order to ease his extremities, and give them up completely to the disposition of the rider. The animal thus finds himself transformed into a kind of balance, of which the rider is the centre piece.

François Baucher: *New Method of Horsemanship*, 1842

It may surprise some readers to find the words of Western rider Pat Parelli ranked alongside those of the great classical riders, the Portugese horseman Oliveira, the early twentieth-century French general, Decarpentry, and the nineteenth-century equestrian innovator, Baucher.

It may be even more of a surprise to find that Baucher, writing in the 1840s, describes the principle of collection in terms that, to all intents and purposes, have become the hallmark of Parelli's Natural Horse-Man-Ship method in the 1990s, or that the cavalryman Decarpentry should list 'caress' as one of the aids. But, as Parelli says elsewhere, 'It's so old, it's new again,' or, to quote a friend, 'What goes around, comes around.'

The four quotations that head this chapter all say something about the ridden aids. They were chosen because it is the interpretation of the aids that is a challenge to every rider: firstly because opinions differ as to what constitutes an aid; and, secondly, because aids can be used in any number of permutations. In spite of this, these four statements, taken collectively, encapsulate everything we need to know about riding, namely:

- The aids can be anything we choose them to be. They are simply cues that stimulate one or more of the horse's senses.
- All aids can produce a partial physical response in the horse. But only some (used in the right combination) stimulate a physical chain of events that makes optimum use of the horse's anatomy, to the rider's advantage.
- The most important of these is the rider's leg aid.
- It is not necessary to memorize lots of different applications of the same aid. It is more important to understand the single principle.

This leads to greater flexibility on the part of the rider.

Aids are a means of communication. It's as simple as that. But such is the horse's ability to pick out cues from the general fuzziness of human behaviour that it's possible for us to choose a completely random set of stimuli in order to teach our horses to do more or less anything. And that is the problem. It's quite feasible to get a horse to perform the right movement for the wrong reason. This doesn't particularly matter, as long as he's not in danger of making the wrong use of his anatomy. The only way to insure against the latter is to understand how the aids work and to know which are most likely to be favourable to the horse's natural way of moving.

In most cases, the ridden aids (as opposed to the cues we might invent for ourselves) have to be learnt, either from an instructor, or from a knowledgeable horse-person. But there are two ways of learning any subject. It doesn't matter whether it's an intellectual subject, such as a science or a language, or a manual skill, such as operating a machine or playing a game. The first way is to learn hundreds of instructions, and follow them. The second way is to learn a handful of facts, and *understand* them.

The first way works well enough if you have the right sort of memory. But it only works reliably as long as you stay within the boundaries set by those instructions. For example, imagine you have been given instructions to get from a street in the suburb to the centre of town. As long as you remember the exact sequence of left and right turns, you will undoubtedly reach your destination. But what happens if you forget one instruction, or make a mistake. With no basic knowledge of the area you have nothing to back up your memory.

If, however, you choose the second way, you might know something about the geography of the town – it doesn't have to be much – you might know roughly the direction you need to go in (north or south, for example), and you

might perhaps have seen a landmark, a river, a church tower, or a railway. You can, by all means, get a set of instructions as well, but it won't be a compete disaster if you forget or lose them.

Mastering the ridden aids is just the same. There are plenty of books, for example, that tell the rider what to do with his legs, seat, and hands, to get the horse to walk, trot, and canter. There are plenty of books that tell the rider how many hoof beats should characterize each gait, and whether the hooves should land on two or more tracks, depending on whether the horse is moving in a straight line, bending on a circle, or yielding sidewards. But these are just lists of instructions. They don't explain 'why' or, more importantly, 'why not'.

What, then, becomes an issue, is the exact way in which the legs, seat (or, more correctly, weight), and the hands are used to get the desired effect. And what is the desired effect, anyway? Do we press constantly with the legs, do we keep the legs in firm contact with the horse's sides at all times, do we keep the legs away from the horse's sides until we have something to say? Do we hold the hands at our waist, hold them out in front of us, hold them six inches apart, or press the knuckles together? I have seen the same horseman put all of these things into practice, at different times, and to good effect. But why? What did he hope to achieve by employing so many different tactics? Could it be that he was responding to the changing needs of his horse, that, as the horse progressed through his work, the rider had to re-establish the best line of communication?

General Decarpentry, in his description of the leg aids, writes:

> To produce impulsion the legs always act by brief contacts with the horse's body. Any prolongation of this contact, any pressure with or without increase in strength, is detrimental to the creation or the development of impulsion… The taps should never be prolonged, but as elastic as those of a spring hammer on an electric bell.

The General goes on to say that even subtler effects of the rider's leg can be obtained by using miniscule actions of the calf muscles. He also concedes that the impact of the leg would be greater if it were brought further away from the horse before 'striking'. However, he then underlines the fact that the small increase in power gained by this means is a bad trade-off against the rider's loss of balance.

Unfortunately, what the General doesn't say is that there is actually a sound physiological reason for using the leg in the way he describes. It goes to the very heart of what we call 'the aids'. The General is really describing the way in which the nerves behave. Not the nerves of the rider, which, of course, operate the rider's calf muscles, but the nerves of the horse, which lie under the rider's legs, in the muscles between each of the ribs.

If you press, even with your fingertips, against the horse's side – preferably in the fleshy space between the ribs – you will notice that the horse flexes away from you. He does so because sensory nerve endings warn him about the pressure, and the motor nerves convert this warning into evasive action. The nerves between the ribs (intercostal nerves) are the lower branches of a common nerve root which also sends fibres to the back muscles. In addition to nerves in the intercostal spaces, there are more superficial nerves which radiate horizontally across the sides of the chest, and which originate from under the shoulder. These are the thoracius nerves (longus, dorsalis, and lateralis).

If we think about it, it is structurally impossible for the horse to 'flinch' his side away from pressure without involving a small section of his back muscles. Therefore, if we apply the pressure from one side only, we get lateral flexion, or bend. (In the middle third of the chest, it's just the hint of bend because the spine itself has limited flexibility. Nevertheless, the heads of the ribs move, and the back muscles contract, and that's a start.)

Now imagine what would happen if we could press our fingers on both sides of the ribcage at once. Obviously, the horse can't 'flinch' both ways simultaneously. So the combined reaction produces lift. The chest, including the spine, can't do anything else, It has nowhere else to go.

This movement, this lifting of the chest cavity in response to pressure from the rider's legs, is the most fundamental ingredient of riding. It is the key to everything that follows, both in terms of the horse's anatomy and in terms of the sequential application of the rider's aids. This, and nothing else, is the passport to impulsion, the gateway to lightness. Understanding the importance of the rider's legs is to have, at once, discovered the Theory of Everything.

Let us return for a moment to nerve physiology. We have to ask ourselves what happens to a nerve – or a muscle which contains a number of nerves – when we press on it continuously. The answer is, it goes numb. That's because nerves work on a series of electrical transmissions that bound along the nerve fibres at intervals. If we simply press and press, and carry on pressing, we overload the transmission: we don't allow the nerve time to clear itself of one set of impulses before it's ready to receive the next.

The time span between impulses is very short, measured only in seconds. Nevertheless, the difference between legs that 'massage' the horse's sides, and legs that try to squeeze the life out of them, is the difference between a horse that can produce an elastic stride and one that produces nothing at all. In other words, the General's recommendation for brief contacts with the legs (though not, of course, flapping them visibly up and down) is nothing less than the correct interpretation of nerve function.

Why is the application of the leg aid so important? Well, for two reasons. The first has to do with the space under the horse's belly. The second is because of the peculiar arrangement of tissues under the horse's shoulders. Let's look a little more closely at what happens when the rider closes his legs against the horse.

The spinal nerves are arranged segmentally along the horse's back. Each nerve has an upper and lower branch, one that innervates the back muscles and one that innervates the intercostal and abdominal muscles. The action of the rider's leg initiates a series of bracing effects around the circumference of the horse's body, as the reflex action of the muscles tries to move the body away from pressure. Imagine the horse's body as a series of slices: it depends on where the rider's leg is placed as to which slice is most intensely affected.

If the rider's leg rests against the tenth or eleventh intercostal space, then the corresponding slice of the intercostal and back muscles will brace the spine here. If the rider's leg moves further back, it will have a greater influence on the abdominal muscles and on the area of the back towards the rear of the saddle, and beyond. If the rider's leg moves further forward, it will have more and more effect on the thoracius nerves, which are extensions of the brachial plexus. (The brachial plexus is the foundation of all the nerves that serve the forelegs.) Therefore, if the leg is at its furthest point forward, it is likely to affect only the action of the forelegs since the chest is already braced between the shoulder blades and cannot do much more. (Remember, these locations are only approximate: much depends on the conformation of the horse.)

Although the bracing mechanism acts most intensely where the rider's leg is situated, it is not confined to this area. The effect spreads to the front and rear of this position, in what should be a continuous arc. The result is that the horse uses his combined chest, abdominal, and back muscles to lift his body. This clears a space under the belly: the space he needs in order to bring his hind legs underneath him. This is the first step towards impulsion and the greater engagement of the hind legs.

The position of the hind legs has a significant effect on what happens at the other end of the horse's body. The hind limbs have to be able to flex and extend in order to raise the body mass, as well as propel it forwards. If the hind legs are placed too far forwards, the strain of flexion is born by the lower joints

(hock and fetlock). Placed too far back they constantly push the body into a nose-dive. Therefore, as a direct result of the rider's leg aid, the hind limbs have the capacity to make or break the horse's forehand.

When God first made the horse, He probably didn't intend him to be ridden. That was a later idea and, we have to say, a good one. But by the time human beings wanted to ride, the anatomy of the horse's forehand was already past the design stage, and they just had to make the best of it.

There are two problems with the horse's forehand. The first is the contour of the spine. It makes a curious dip under the shoulder blades, at the place where the neck vertebrae end and the thoracic vertebrae begin. This is the area in front of the first rib. The second is the attachment of the forelimbs. They have no bony fixation to the main frame; they are suspended by muscles.

In the natural, non-ridden horse, there is an advantage to this anatomical arrangement. The curve of the spine in the area in front of the first rib gives the horse enormous flexibility of movement through the base of the neck, from 'head down' for grazing, to 'head up' for watching, listening, posturing, and generally expressing himself. For this reason, the musculature at the base of the neck falls into two distinct systems. On the one band, there are the powerful neck muscles, which span the distance from the shoulders to the base of the skull and from the breast bone to the jaw. On the other band, there are smaller muscles, in close proximity to the spine, which leap-frog their way up the neck without giving a great deal of support to the individual vertebrae. The base of the neck is designed to have a high degree of mobility; it was never meant to be a load-bearing structure.

Many of the neck muscles – those that produce wonderful girations of movement in the horse at liberty – originate not on bone but on fascia. This fascia is situated under, and lies parallel with, the horse's shoulder blades. The shoulder blades themselves are attached to the body by means of a fan-shaped arrangement of muscles (the 'fingers' of the serratus ventralis muscle). This lies over the fascia. The movement of the forelegs is generated from approximately the top third portion of the shoulder blades.

Anybody who has watched a horse on high alert, trotting or prancing round his paddock, will know that he does so with elevation. He uses his body, and especially the base of his neck, to enhance his posture by lifting his forehand. What he is also doing is protecting the area of the spine under the shoulders. He needs to do this, because the anatomy here is vulnerable: it's the place of origin of the brachial plexus.

The nerves of the brachial plexus, which exit the spinal cord between each of the last three neck vertebrae and the first three thoracic vertebrae, are made up of a criss-cross of nerve fibres. These form the nerves that serve the front legs – from the shoulders right down to the horse's toes.

Without lift, the base of the neck has to rely, for postural support, on the large neck muscles. Without lift, the neck vertebrae in front of the first rib remain dipped because they have next to no support of their own. If the horse's head carriage is high, they may even be actively forced down. Without lift, the fascia bears the brunt of impulsion from the hind legs, and the brachial plexus bears the consequence. Of course, the horse can lift himself, but what is responsible for this lift when the horse is ridden? That responsibility falls to the rider's legs.

Once the rider has established lift by the correct pressure of the legs (what we call 'the supporting leg') every other aid is subsidiary and serves only to fine-tune the horse's movements. As the horse lifts through the base of the neck, or, as some people say, comes up through the withers, the curve at the base of the neck vertebrae opens out and produces a reciprocal tipping forwards at the top of the neck. The poll becomes the highest point (con-formation allowing) and the head tips down from the poll. If the chest/neck junction is operating correctly, the head can't do anything else. The rider's hands do not need to adjust the horse's head, the head position adjusts the rider's hands,

The same can be said of the rider's seat. Nowadays, we talk about 'seat' whereas the old masters talked of weight, which is much more realistic. In fact, the seat is not the rider's, it is the horse's. If the horse does not brace his body under the rider's weight, then the rider has nothing to sit on. The rider is totally ineffective, and he cannot therefore be said to have a seat. Conversely, if the rider applies his body too forcefully, or at the wrong position, he cancels out the advantage he has gained by using his legs. So he still doesn't have a seat. It is the subtle and strategic use of weight that is the real aid. As the French horseman General L'Hotte expressed it, the rider's seat should only give him the feeling of riding on the 'gentle waves of a quiet lake'.

To summarize, the aids are exactly what they say they are: aids. They help the rider communicate with his horse. Almost anything can be an aid. It doesn't have to be just legs and hands, it can be the click of the tongue, an intake of breath, a particular corner of the indoor school, or the conveniently placed hedgerow that you encounter while out on a quiet hack. They are just cues that we humans use to support our message to the horse, and the horse quickly learns to recognize these cues as a request for some sort of response.

However, of all the possible cues we can dream up (and there have been many over the centuries), it's only the rider's legs (which generate impulsion) and the rider's hands (which regulate impulsion), that have a substantial and consistent effect on the horse's anatomy, an effect that automatically comes with a built-in safety-net for the horse's forehand. It just so happens that this effect coincides exactly with what we now call the classical way of riding.

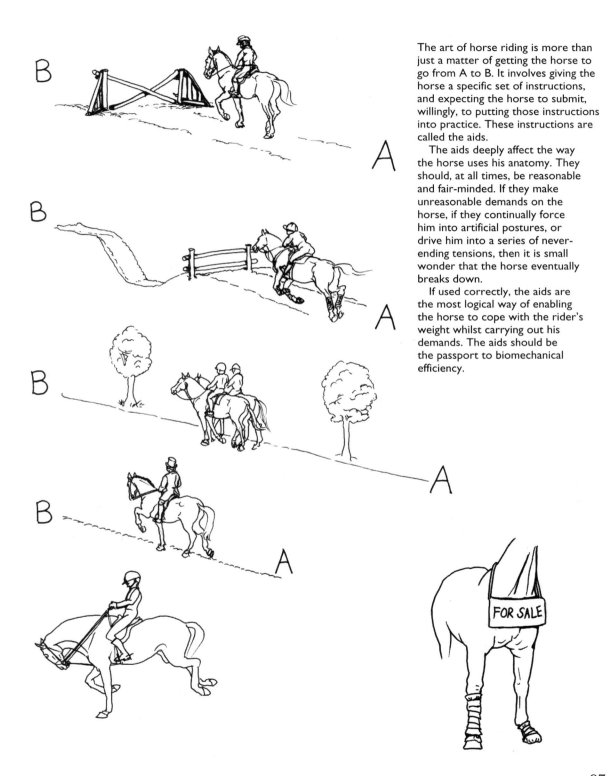

The art of horse riding is more than just a matter of getting the horse to go from A to B. It involves giving the horse a specific set of instructions, and expecting the horse to submit, willingly, to putting those instructions into practice. These instructions are called the aids.

The aids deeply affect the way the horse uses his anatomy. They should, at all times, be reasonable and fair-minded. If they make unreasonable demands on the horse, if they continually force him into artificial postures, or drive him into a series of never-ending tensions, then it is small wonder that the horse eventually breaks down.

If used correctly, the aids are the most logical way of enabling the horse to cope with the rider's weight whilst carrying out his demands. The aids should be the passport to biomechanical efficiency.

97

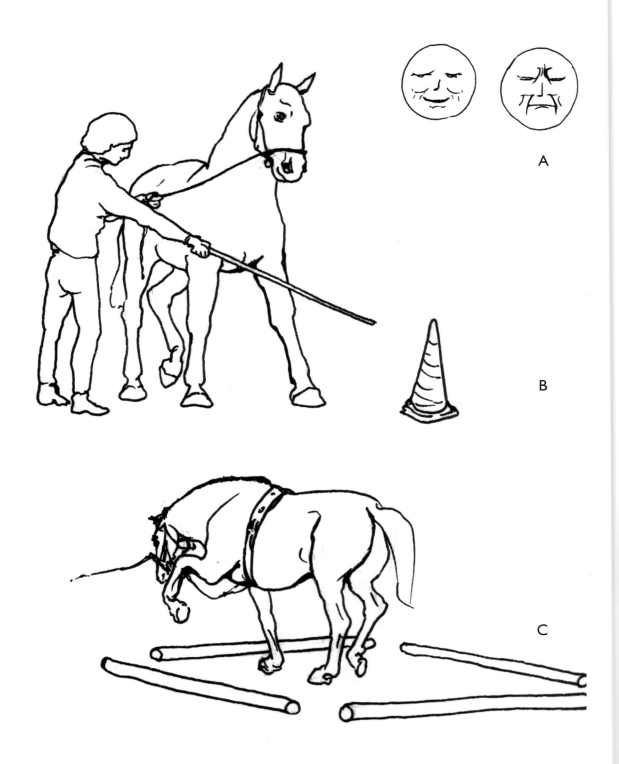

A

B

C

Aids in the making.

In the strictest sense, the aids consist of different combinations of physical stimuli applied by the rider to strategic, and particularly sensitive (or sensitized) parts of the horse's body. In reality, the aids are much more than this. They depend on our state of mind, on our emotions (A). These affect the way we breathe, which, in itself, is acutely registered by the horse. The way we breathe affects the state of relaxation, or tension, in our muscles and joints.

Apart from purely physical intervention by the rider, aids can be more or less anything we want them to be. At the most basic level, they are simply cues to which the horse replies with a learned response. They may, or may not, teach the horse to use his body in a way that is biomechanically efficient for the purpose of being ridden.

For example, behavioural training (B) allows the horse to raise his level of self-confidence by encouraging him to make his own decisions, and act on them. This may help him mentally in his ridden training, and the mental process may help to improve his posture. But, it doesn't, per se, put him 'on the bit', or 'in front of the leg' – only perhaps by association.

Lungeing and long-reining (C), with or without postural 'gadgets', and visual stimuli such as poles on the ground, can imitate some of the stimuli otherwise given by the rider. But they are a less reliable means of getting the horse to consistently lift and support his back than, for example, the aid given by the rider's legs.

The purest form of the aid is one where muscle speaks to muscle (D): the rider's leg to the horse's side, the rider's hand to the horse's mouth, and the rider's weight to the horse's back. But such purity would be sterile, and it does not leave room for the power of human imagination. In fact, each aid consists of a simple reflex action, combined with a more complex process of learning based on any number of stimuli of our devising. That's what makes riding both fascinating and individual!

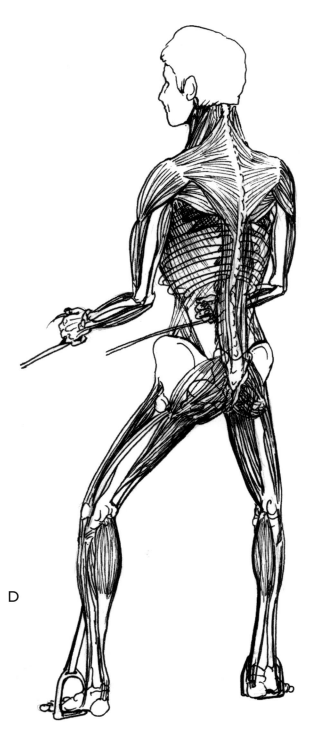

D

99

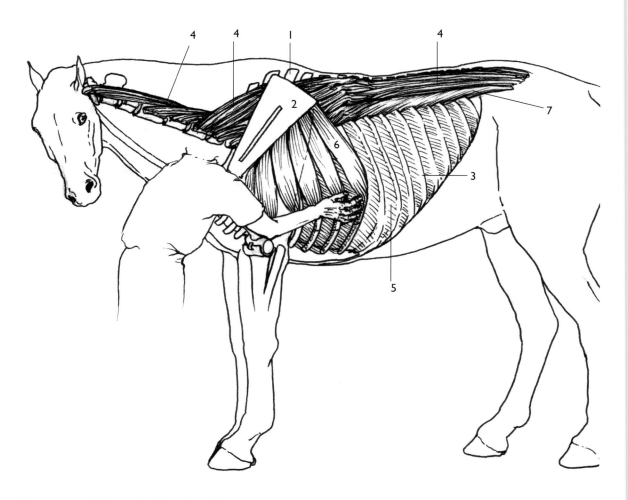

If we press on the horse's side with our fingers, we can activate a reflex, which involves not only the local area of skin and muscle under our fingers, but also a precise area of the horse's back.

In effect, the pressure stretches part of a muscle, which causes the body to adjust the length by instructing the muscle to contract. In this instance, the hand is pressing against nerves that have a common root with nerves that serve the long back muscles. In the same way that if you or I received a sudden dig in the ribs we would flinch away using part of our spine, the horse similarly tries to relieve the pressure, momentarily recoiling, by using a corresponding segment of the back.

This is a simple reflex, which produces a small degree of lateral flexion. If the stimulus is short and sharp, the horse will react abruptly. If the stimulus is gradual, the response will likewise be more graded and sustained. In other words, the stimulus, in this case pressure, can be metered out to create exactly the desired effect. All that is required is consistent (and gentle) reinforcement at one site. There is nothing to be gained by continually changing the point of pressure.

If it were possible to use our fingers to press on both sides of the horse simultaneously, we would then produce bilateral flexion. But, because it is impossible for the spine to flex in opposite directions at the same time, this bilateral pressure produces lift. The lift of the spine by the back muscles has the effect of bracing the horse's back under the weight of the rider. It provides a well-sprung seat for him to sit on.

100

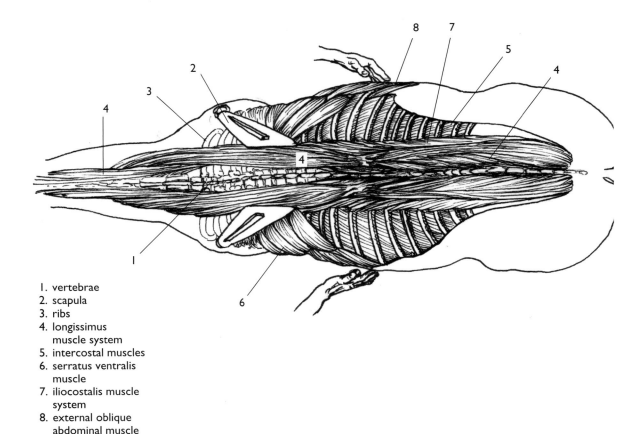

1. vertebrae
2. scapula
3. ribs
4. longissimus
   muscle system
5. intercostal muscles
6. serratus ventralis
   muscle
7. iliocostalis muscle
   system
8. external oblique
   abdominal muscle

The back muscles consist of a deep layer of short muscles that span the short spaces between each of the vertebrae, and a superficial layer of long muscles (longissimus and iliocostalis muscles) that leap-frog their way up the spine from the hindquarters to the head. The long muscles pick up attachments from the dorsal and transverse processes of the vertebrae en route. In this sense, the construction of the long back muscles is as segmental as that of the short ones. Both are innervated, at the same regular Intervals, by branches of the same nerves.

But, for the purpose of riding, it is important to think of the long back muscles as having a single span, a span that continues without interruption under the shoulders. The effect of lifting the back by activating the intercostal reflex should not, under any circumstance, be confined to a single segment of the body. It should involve the entire length of the spine, especially that part at the base of the neck, in front of the first rib.

In order to achieve a uniform bracing of the horse's spine, the exact location of the pressure in relation to the length of the back is very important.

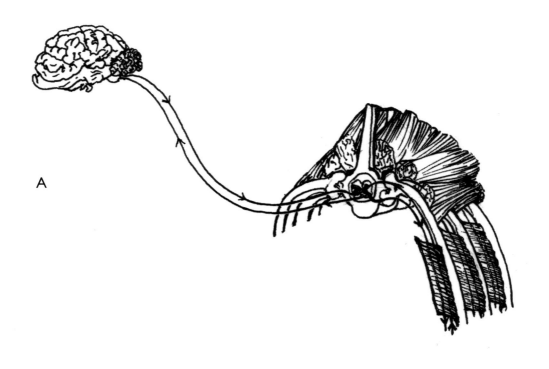

A

B

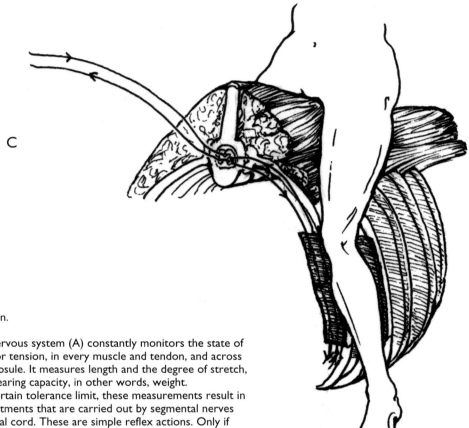

C

Proprioception.

The body's nervous system (A) constantly monitors the state of contraction, or tension, in every muscle and tendon, and across every joint capsule. It measures length and the degree of stretch, or the load-bearing capacity, in other words, weight.

Within a certain tolerance limit, these measurements result in postural adjustments that are carried out by segmental nerves along the spinal cord. These are simple reflex actions. Only if the postural changes involve conscious decision-making do the messages have to travel as far as the brain itself.

We all need proprioception to help us orientate ourselves in our environment. The horse uses his to manoeuvre through different spatial arrangements and over various obstacles (B). Although, fundamentally, both horses and humans use proprioception to tell them which way up the world is, the effect of this information is different, depending on whether you walk on four legs, or two.

When we sit on the horse's back (C), and begin to apply pressure to his skin and muscles, we change the tension across these structures: we interfere with the horse's proprioception. The horse has to reply with a postural change, which can be anything from a small nod to a grand gesture.

If we imagine that the stimulus we give the horse is the equivalent of an 'invitation to the dance', then we can expect, by way of a reply, anything from a simple affirmative from the spinal cord to a tempestuous outburst from the brain. It all depends on the intensity of our input in relation to the horse's level of training and/or his natural sensitivity.

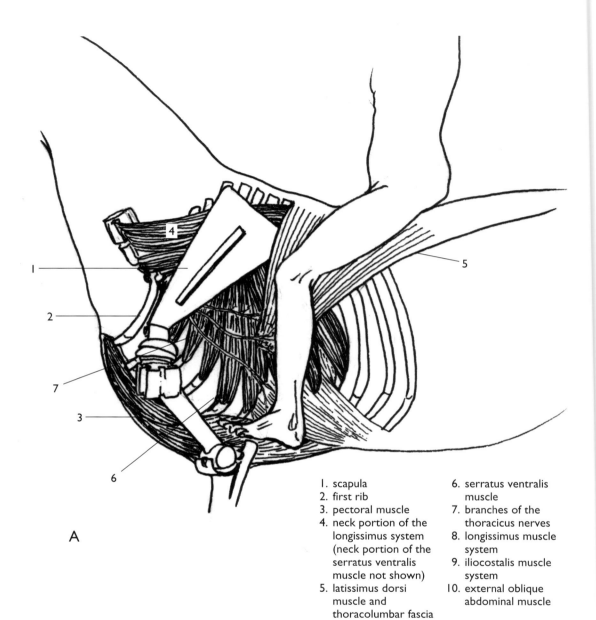

A

1. scapula
2. first rib
3. pectoral muscle
4. neck portion of the longissimus system (neck portion of the serratus ventralis muscle not shown)
5. latissimus dorsi muscle and thoracolumbar fascia
6. serratus ventralis muscle
7. branches of the thoracicus nerves
8. longissimus muscle system
9. iliocostalis muscle system
10. external oblique abdominal muscle

The position of the rider's leg.

If the rider's lower leg is too far forward in relation to his body (A), it will press on muscles more related to the suspension of the front of the rib than on those that help to brace the horse's back.

There are long nerve extensions (the thoracicus nerves) that stem from the brachial plexus under the shoulders. These innervate the serratus ventralis, deep pectoral, and part of the latissimus dorsi muscles. If the rider stimulates these muscles, he is reinforcing the muscular suspension of the forehand rather than supporting the back. The chest muscles cannot lift the spine; they only prevent it from being jarred.

The effect of the leg in this position may produce a more extravagant forelimb stride, but it does so at the expense of a well-braced back. The long back muscles are not in the equation

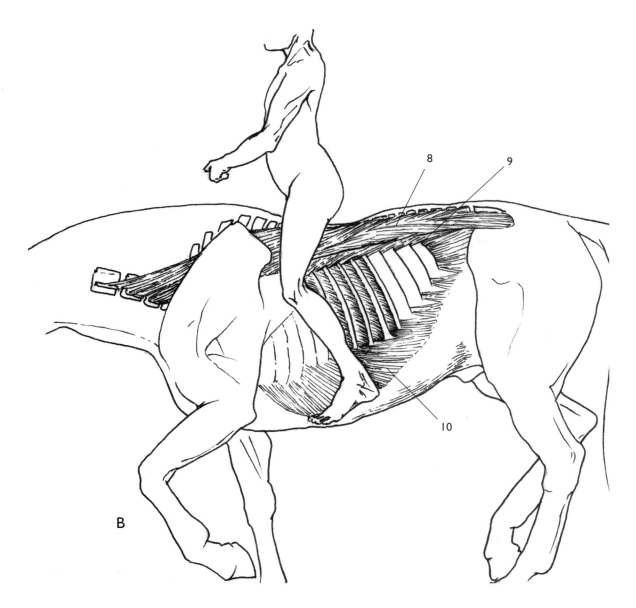

because the effect of the leg is diminished through the layers of chest muscles. The lengthened forelimb stride will apply some traction to the latissimus dorsi muscle (insertion on the shoulder muscles can't be shown here), and this will increase the support of the lower back by the thoracolumbar fascia. But that is all. To all intents and purposes, this rider is a passenger – and an uncomfortable one at that.

If the rider's leg is too far back in relation to his body (B), he will stimulate the horse's abdominal muscles. This will reinforce the support of the back muscles in the region of the lumbar spine, which is in fact used to a degree in lateral movements. However, when the horse is moving in a straight line, the effect is too localized. It does not empower the long back muscles to support the spine as far forward as the base of the horse's neck.

The rider himself is out of balance: he is on the forehand, and so is his horse.

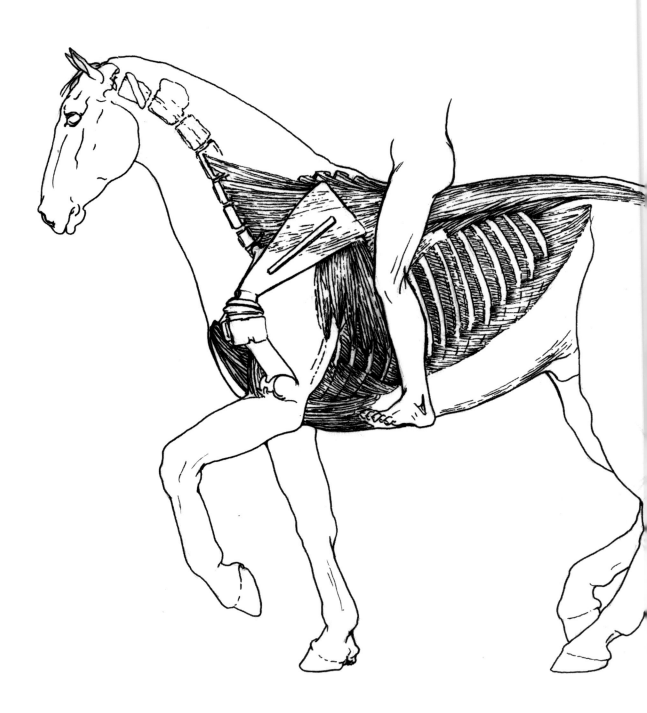

Creating a seat.

When the rider's leg is beneath his own body weight then firstly, he himself is in balance – as if he was standing on the ground – and, secondly, he is applying the leg aid to the muscles directly underneath his body.

He is not using his seat, he's creating one!

From the buttocks and thigh down, the rider's leg folds itself around the horse, encompassing the small spinal muscles, the long back muscles, and the intercostal muscles. These are wrapped around by the latissimus dorsi muscle and the thoracolumbar fascia. The latissimus dorsi feeds into the medial muscles of the shoulder, while the fascia gives a plastic contour to the muscles of the lower back.

In this position the rider's lower leg can address the abdominal muscles (rear hand suspension) or the chest muscles (forehand suspension), in varying degrees, without losing his balance. The back is braced In a continuous arc because of the strategic, central application of the aid.

The 'all-round' suspension created by stimulating the muscles in the mid-back, directly beneath the rider's body, immediately takes the pressure off the bones at the base of the neck in the area in front of the first rib. The horse can, literally, come up through the withers. The forehand no longer weighs heavily on the pectoral sling, and the neck muscles do not drag on the fascia that is buried deep beneath the shoulders.

The combined response of back, chest and abdomen to the rider's leg in this position lifts the horse's body and creates space under the belly. From here it is a small step to increase the activity of the horse's hind legs and raise the forehand, which is the beginning of collection.

When the rider sits in balance and the horse supports himself, in balance, both horse and rider come very close to sharing the same proprioceptive horizon. The communication that takes place between horse and rider is then extremely refined. It is based exclusively on a language of muscle to muscle interaction, and needs no additional stimuli to be effective.

In terms of sustainability, this is the most effective and biomechanically economic way of riding there is.

In showjumping and cross-country jumping, there are special considerations of balance and movement that influence the position of the rider's leg. Whether the rider rides 'long' or 'short', the leg still has to be effective. The calf, heel, or spur pressure acts on the nerves, around the horse's sides, that correspond to strategic parts of his back. The pressure is applied at the middle portion of the muscle/nerve complex, rather than at a point further away from the horse's spine (as, for example, in dressage).

In jumping, it is just as important for the leg to be under the rider's body for the same reasons that apply to dressage: for back support. But the shorter stirrup length used for jumping allows the rider to free the horse's lower back, as the situation demands, while maintaining his own sense of balance.

As long as the rider's leg is in a position to lift the horse underneath him, any length of stirrup can be used without sacrificing part of the horse's biomechanical efficiency. The rider simply has to keep returning to the basic position of vertical alignment – a line from the ear, through the shoulder, through the hip, and down to the ankle – even if it is only for a few strides between jumps.

Without due support from the rider's leg, all the grim determination in the world will not produce more impulsion from a horse. If the rider does not create a seat for himself, the back muscles cannot lift and brace the spine. Strain is caused to the attachments of the long back muscles at the croup, and at the base of the neck.

The area of the spine in front of the first rib is supported by relatively slender muscles that form a cross-bracing in close proximity to the vertebrae. The bones have fan-like ligamentous attachments to the nuchal ligament, which are sandwiched between layers of fascia and then encased in the heavy-duty neck muscles. This is an area of high mobility; it's also the area where the roots of the brachial plexus are to be found.

At the other end of the horse, the junction between the lumbar spine and the sacrum is the area of maximum impulsion, rather than sheer 'bend-ability' as in the neck. This intersection has to allow for the angle of the pelvis to become steeper as the muscles of the hindquarters push the body forwards, without allowing the spinal cord to be squashed in the process. The survival of the spine and spinal cord depend heavily on the protective support of the back muscles and fascia.

The sacroiliac joint – the attachment of the pelvis to the sacrum – is not designed to move at all. It provides the bony foundation for the seamless transmission of forces from the thigh muscles to the muscles of the quarters and the lower back.

When the horse runs onto the forehand, the impact of his own bodyweight and that of the rider is thrown onto the vital structures at the base of the neck – for example, the cervical attachments of the longissimus muscle. The latissimus dorsi muscle braces the forehand to save it from jarring, but this transfers the problem back to the thoracolumbar fascia. The muscles behind the saddle become tense as they, too, try to reduce the impact on the forehand. This, in turn, prevents the horse from engaging his hindquarters and increasing the stride length of his hind legs.

1. cervical portion of the longissimus muscle system
2. lumbar portion of the longissimus muscle system
3. latissimus dorsi muscle
4. fascia

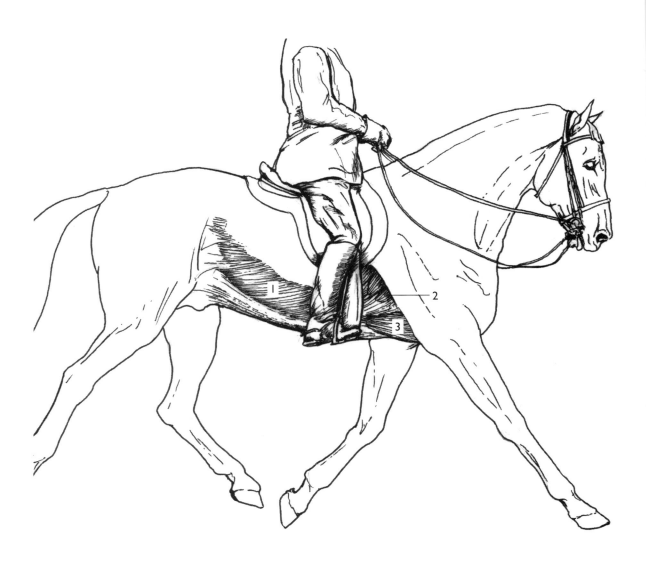

When the rider's leg is in the optimum position, it not only braces the horse's spine through the intercostal reflex but it rests against end portions of the external oblique abdominal muscle. The abdominal support created by this muscle, and the underlying abdominal muscles, contributes to the sustained support of the back (the reciprocal action of spine and abdominal muscles has been likened to that of the bow and bowstring.)

The abdominal lift creates space under the horse's belly. This is the space he needs in order to increase the stride length of the hind legs. The more space, the greater his potential to engage the hind legs. The space beneath the horse is the source of his impulsion.

As the hind legs become more active, the hips become lower, and the back more rounded. This enables the horse to take the weight off the forehand, which immediately relieves the pressure on the structures at the base of the neck.

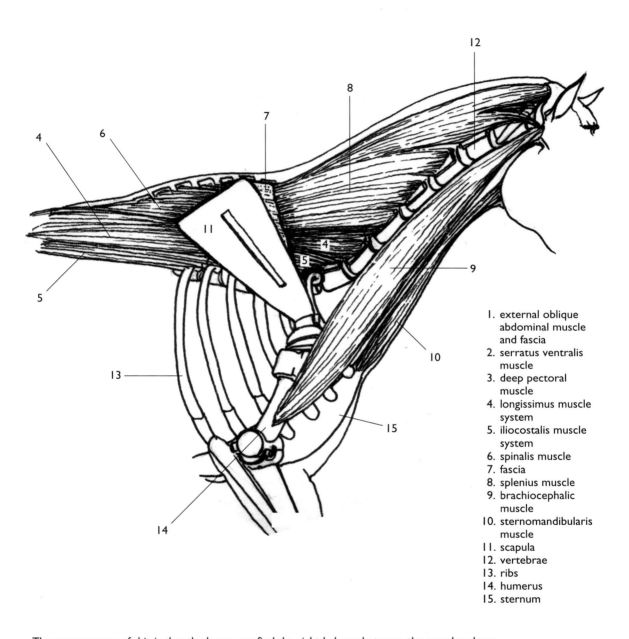

1. external oblique
   abdominal muscle
   and fascia
2. serratus ventralis
   muscle
3. deep pectoral
   muscle
4. longissimus muscle
   system
5. iliocostalis muscle
   system
6. spinalis muscle
7. fascia
8. splenius muscle
9. brachiocephalic
   muscle
10. sternomandibularis
    muscle
11. scapula
12. vertebrae
13. ribs
14. humerus
15. sternum

The consequence of this is that the horse can find the right balance between the muscles along the top of the neck and those along the bottom. For example, the splenius muscle, which originates in the fascia deep under the shoulder blades, counterbalances the brachiocephalic muscle, which originates on the humerus bone, and the sternomandibularis muscle, which originates on the breastbone. These muscles (though not exclusively) combine their effect to determine the position of the head, in accordance with the posture dictated by the forehand. This posture is determined by the abdominal lift and the support of the back, all of which are a direct consequence of the rider's leg. This is the foundation of self-carriage.

The effect of the rider's leg is to initiate a sequence of anatomical responses in the horse which logically, and inevitably, lead to impulsion, self-carriage and ultimately collection.

To summarize, the leg:

- Braces the back through the back muscles and thoracolumbar fascia;
- Sustains the support of the back by engaging the abdominal muscles;
- Creates space under the horse's body for the hind legs to step into;
- Relieves the tissues close to the spine in the area of the first rib, as well as the muscles at the base of the neck;
- Safeguards the nerves to the hindquarters by not straining the thoracolumbar and gluteal fascias;
- Safeguards the nerves to the forelegs by allowing the muscles along the top and bottom of the neck to find their natural equilibrium.

Once the correct anatomical sequence is in place, It becomes obvious that gadgets, such as draw reins, are, at best, superfluous, at worst, inadmissible. If one looks at the muscle structure of the neck, the horse is quite capable of creating his own draw reins if he is so minded.

The only case for gadgets is if the horse has learned to take advantage of the rider because the aids were previously inadequate, inappropriate, or unclear. Then a skilled horseman might be justified in using a gadget to break a habit, as long as one dependence is not simply substituted for another!

A. The rider occupies a very small area of the horse's body, but the effects of his legs reach from the horse's head to his toes.

B. The abdominal lift lightens the forehand.

C. Balance and counterbalance. The muscles of the neck determine the position of the head. But they must do so as a consequence of the forehand posture, not in spite of it.

D. The use of draw reins is largely a nonsense. The horse is quite capable of using his own muscles to this effect, although it would probably give him a tension headache if he did so for very long.

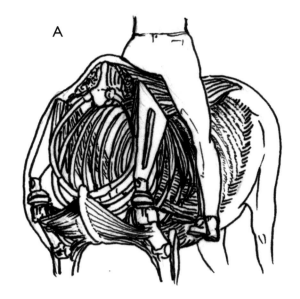

A

C

B

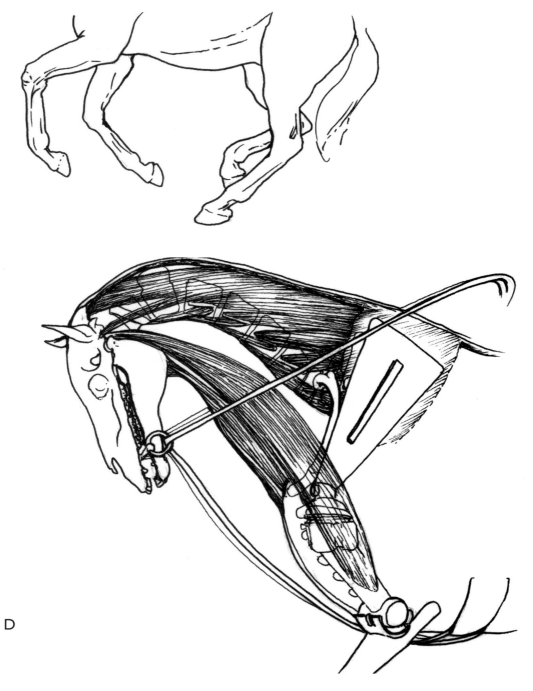

D

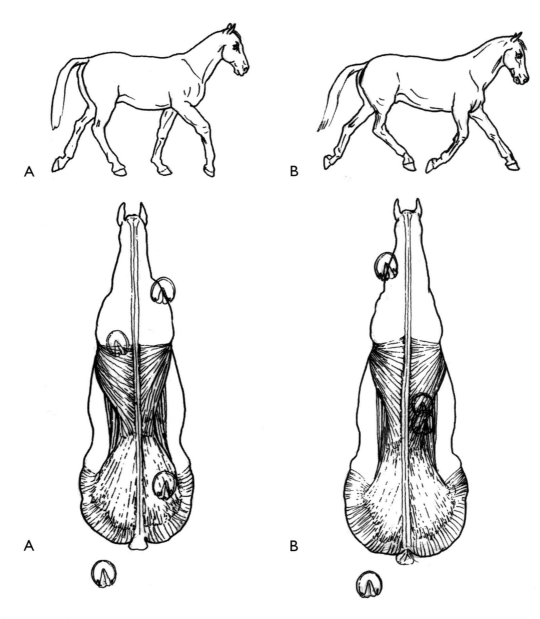

A bird's-eye view of the horse shows the all-embracing effect of the latissimus dorsi muscle and its fascial attachments, which extend as far back as the hindquarters. The narrow central structure running down the length of the horse's body is the nuchal/supraspinous ligament. Both the latissimus dorsi muscle and the thoracolumbar and gluteal fascia connect to this ligament, making their effect felt from the poll to the tail.

The gaits of the horse are generally classified as walk, trot, canter and gallop. These are subdivided into working, medium, and extended paces. This segregation is an oversimplification of the variety of steps and rhythms that the horse uses. For example, if you watch top-class showjumping horses in the confines of an indoor arena – where there are big fences, all with related distances – the gait is often a hybrid movement, a mixture of strides from the fore and hind limbs, somewhere between a trot and canter.

116

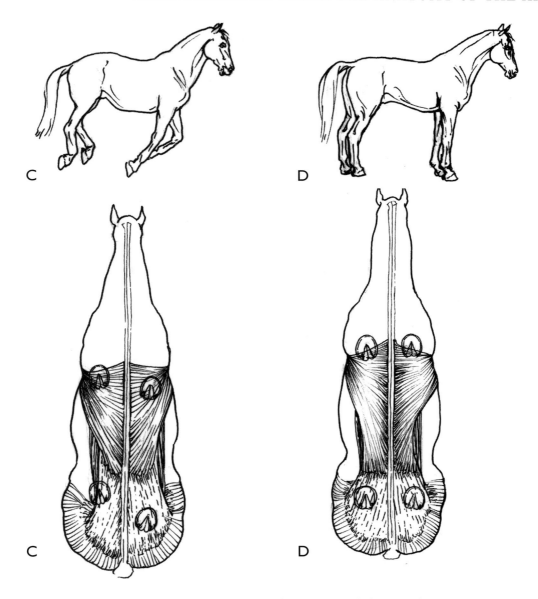

C   D

C   D

In reality, the horse's movements would be better described as a sliding scale from 'stop' to 'very fast', with or without varying degrees of elevation. However, traditionally, and for the purposes of competitions, we need to work within the accepted parameters, which means the horse has to make specific transitions. He has to change between gaits with different foot patterns, different rhythms, and different demands on balance. In order to change smoothly, from one 'gear' to the next, he needs a sound clutch mechanism, and this is the purpose of the latissimus dorsi muscle and the thoracolumbar fascia.

In all transitions between walk (A), trot (B), and canter (C) and especially in the transitions to, and from, the halt (D), the supporting function of these tissues is paramount. They sustain the self-carriage in preparation for the next movement. Anything that impinges on these tissues, such as the downward force of the rider's seat bones, or the rocking motion of a badly fitting saddle, negates any effort by the rider to move his horse forwards (or backwards), smoothly. These tissues are the great unifying features of the horse's movement.

117

The rider has the capacity to stimulate, or interfere with, the transmission of driving power from the quarters to the forehand, using his bodyweight in general, and his seat bones in particular.

Depending on the width of the rider's seat bones in comparison to the breadth of the horse's back, he can apply pressure to the longissimus muscle system, the iliocostalis muscle system, or he can 'pinch' the supraspinous ligament. The rider can allow himself to be carried along by the natural activity of these muscles, he can expand their movement by applying small amounts of intermittent pressure (changing the length of the back muscle for brief moments so that the muscle responds with short bursts of contraction, which gives the forehand greater reach), or he can apply so much downward force that the horse's front and rear become completely disengaged, and the horse can only rattle along like a sewing machine.

1. neck portion of the longissimus muscle system
2. teres major muscle
3. tensor fascia antibrachii muscle
4. latissimus dorsi muscle
5. thoracolumbar and gluteal fascia
6. nuchal/ supraspinous ligament
7. longissimus muscle system
8. iliocastalis muscle system
9. gluteus medius muscle
10. latissimus dorsi muscle
11. fascia
12. gluteal tongue
13. trapezius muscle

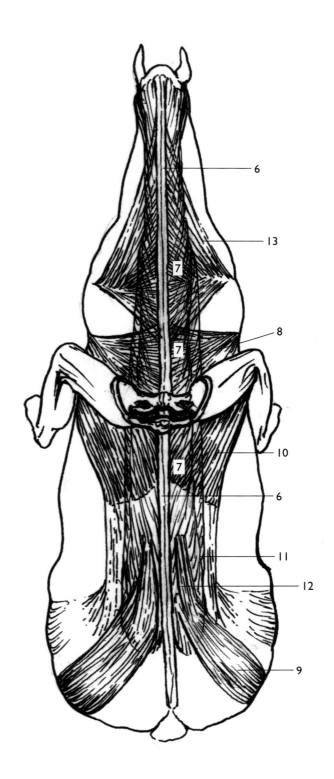

True self-carriage can only come from the horse himself, and then only when his back and abdominal muscles allow the neck to find the most appropriate position as a counterbalance.

Any attempt by the rider's hand to dictate the position of the head and neck must be futile, for the following reason: muscles do not work in isolation. They have synergists (muscles that reinforce their function), and antagonists (muscles that have an opposing function). If, however, we artificially isolate one muscle, or muscle group, and make it so short that it becomes cramped, then any other muscle that is part of the natural sequence of movement becomes blocked. The cramped muscle (or muscles) prevents other muscles from expanding and contracting normally because it has rendered their point of insertion immovable. In other words, if one set of muscles is locked 'short', another dependent set of muscles becomes locked 'long'.

The neck muscles are a functional continuation of the long back muscles. But – in the case of vertical flexion or elevation of the neck – if the neck muscles are locked 'short' then the back muscles will be locked 'long'. The horse's back will be unsupported, and the hind limbs will be unable to engage.

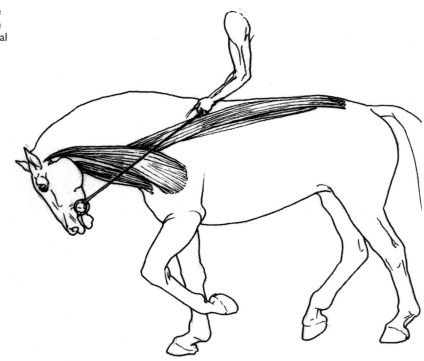

As long as we want to ride in straight lines, it is logical to assume that our aids must be bilaterally equal. However, the moment we want to ask for any degree of lateral flexion, whether it be along the track (in the arena), through a corner, or on a circle, then our body position has to change.

When the horse moves on a circle or through a corner (which is a segment of a circle), he has to bend along the length of his body. Anatomically, the principle is the same whether the circle is 20, 10, or 6 metres in diameter. The horse simply has to adjust the size of his steps to the size of the circle, and the smaller the step the greater the degree of elevation required. The principle also holds good for many of the lateral movements: there again the amount of elevation will increase to allow the horse's limbs to move obliquely under his body.

As the horse begins to turn onto a circle, the support of the fascia (which is like a body stocking of connective tissue) becomes vital. The limbs on the inside of the circle describe a smaller track than those on the outside. If the horse leans into the bend, the small steps become very difficult, and the potential for strain is clear. The horse must have enough clearance under his chest and belly, to the inside of the circle, to allow him to bring the inside legs closer together.

1. (a) nuchal ligament
   (b) supraspinous ligament
2. fascia, origin of splenius muscle
3. fascia, forming a link between the latissimus dorsi muscle round the chest and the bicep femoris muscle of the thigh
4. abdominal fascia and muscle
5. fascia lata, and crural fascia, providing large areas of insertion for all the major muscles of the hind limbs

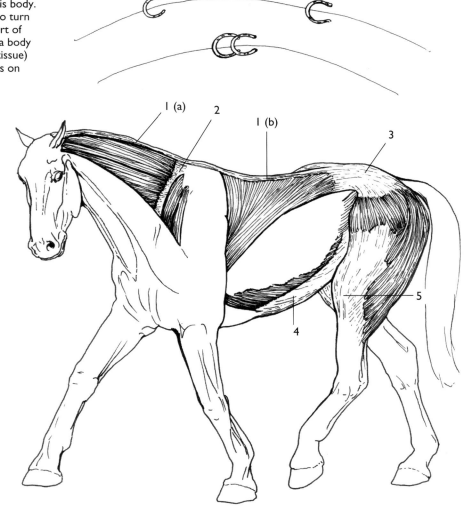

121

The rider's aids for all movements involving lateral length-bend are inter-related and stem from the basic principle that the rider's leg lifts the horse's body underneath him. All that changes is the position of the rider's legs relative to each other, which inevitably changes the position of the rider's pelvis and torso.

The 'steering' with the rider's hands, which always presents a major difficulty on circles and bends, is the most logical consequence of the effect achieved by the legs.

A. When there is no support from the rider's legs, the hands simply pull on the horse's mouth. The horse's head is twisted and, with it, all the muscles that insert on the jaw, side of the skull, and poll. The horse can, to some extent, 'follow his nose', but he places tremendous strain along the whole of his inside length. The muscles stiffen to avoid jarring, and can't provide the elastic lift necessary for him to take small springy steps with the inside legs.

B. The rider's inside leg is positioned to give good support to the inside length of the horse and to encourage lateral flexion. The rider's outside leg is further back, towards the abdomen, to support the outside lumbar muscles and prevent the quarters from swinging out of the bend.

However, the rider's hands are trying to 'steer' the horse as though he were pushing a pram or riding a motorbike. They have created an uncomfortable kink in front of the withers. The inside neck muscles are locked 'short': they are blocking the shoulder. The inside back muscles cannot transfer the momentum from the quarters to the base of the neck, and then up the neck to the poll. They are effectively locked as well, but, in contrast to the neck muscles, the back muscles are locked 'long'. The entire outer length of the horse is also locked long, and there are now only two possibilities: the rider can haul the horse through the bend, or the horse can go out through the shoulder.

C. When the rider supports the outside length of the horse with his leg *and* his hand, the outside muscles form an elastic brace from which the inside muscles can generate the lift necessary to enable the horse to take smaller steps on the inside of the circle. The horse describes two related circles, one slightly larger than the other.

Once the horse has sufficient lift to carry himself through the bend, the rider should be able to dispense with the inside rein and maintain the horse's posture with his legs.

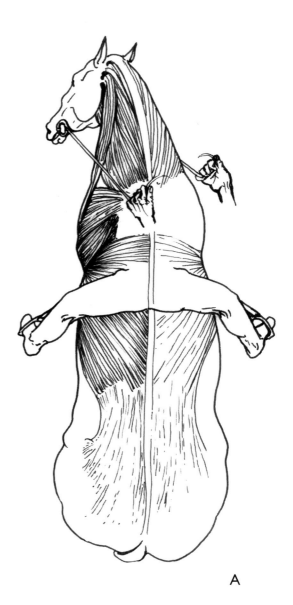

A

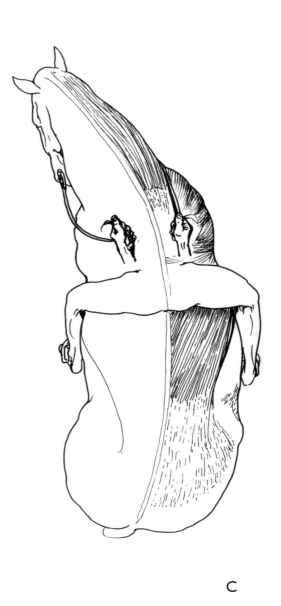

B

C

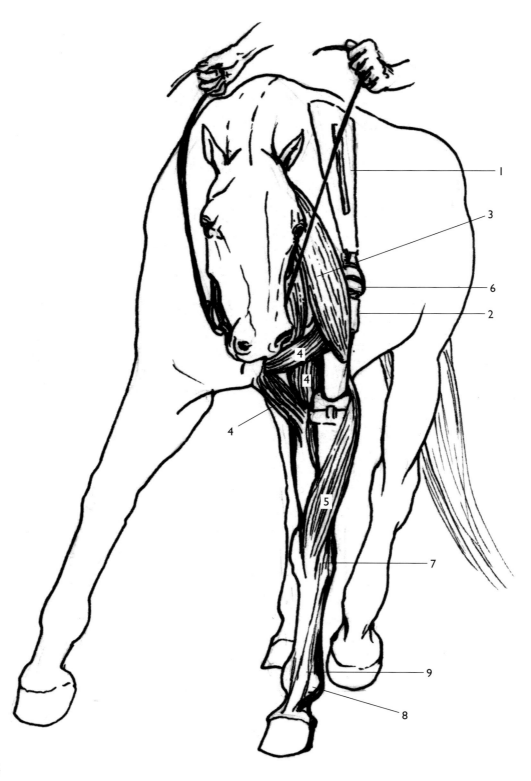

Sowing the seeds of lameness: pulling the horse into the bend with the inside rein.

If the horse's body is to describe a bend, then his inside and outside legs must move on parallel tracks. This can only happen if the muscles along the inside and outside length of the horse work in unison rather than in contradiction.

Of course, the steps on the outside of the bend must be larger because here the circumference of the circle is larger. But this doesn't mean to say that it's only the inside muscles that produce lateral flexion. If the steps on the outside of the bend are too long, the inside of the horse will be racing to keep up with the outside. And because the outside of the horse is straighter, the outside will win.

In order to keep the two sides of the horse parallel, the outside rein must control the outer dimension of the circle. Only then does the inside length of the horse have something to flex against: it can't just flex in isolation. However, if the rider reaches forward with the outside rein and pulls backwards (or backwards and downwards), with the inside rein, the outside of the horse's neck is long, while the inside is cramped. The brachiocephalic muscle, which connects the humerus bone to the side of the skull, is the first muscle to initiate the forwards movement in the foreleg. But it can't do so if it's locked short. If one side is locked short then the same muscle on the other side is locked long. Neither muscle can function correctly: the stride on the inside of the bend will be short and choppy; the stride on the outside of the bend will be long and lopey.

Under these circumstances, the inside foreleg keeps hitting the ground at shorter intervals than the outside foreleg does. The horse responds to this uneven rhythm by bracing the inside base of the neck and the pectoral muscles, inevitably making the situation worse. Because the shortened step is on the inside of the circle, the body weight is thrown more heavily onto the lateral side of the forelimb as it hits the ground. The impact of the stride acts on all the ligaments along the lateral edges of the joints, especially those of the shoulder, knee and fetlock joints.

Riding the horse correctly through a bend is one of the most difficult procedures because the concept of turning on a bend is vastly different between horses and humans. If the horse at liberty wants to turn on a bend, he does so using the whole length of his body. Or, if he wishes simply to turn his neck in one direction whilst moving in another, he increases his elevation. If the human wants to turn on a bend, he can do so by swivelling from the waist upwards. He thinks nothing of it, because his muscles and spine are designed to do so. However, this innate ability can easily put him at cross purposes with the horse, especially on the left rein. This is where human righthandness becomes the undoing of the circle: the right side of the human body tries to 'help' the left side by oversteering.

Whatever the figure to be ridden, the rider's shoulders should remain parallel to the shoulders of the horse. If they are, and if the elbows retain the same flexed position so that there is an uninterrupted line along the rein from the rider's hand to the horse's mouth, then (with the correct support of the legs) the system is in place to describe a perfect circle. All that matters is the size.

1. scapula
2. humerus
3. brachiocephalic
   muscle
4. superficial and deep
   pectoral muscles
5. extensor carpi
   radialis muscle
6. shoulder joint
7. carpus (knee)
8. fetlock joint
9. common digital
   extensor tendon

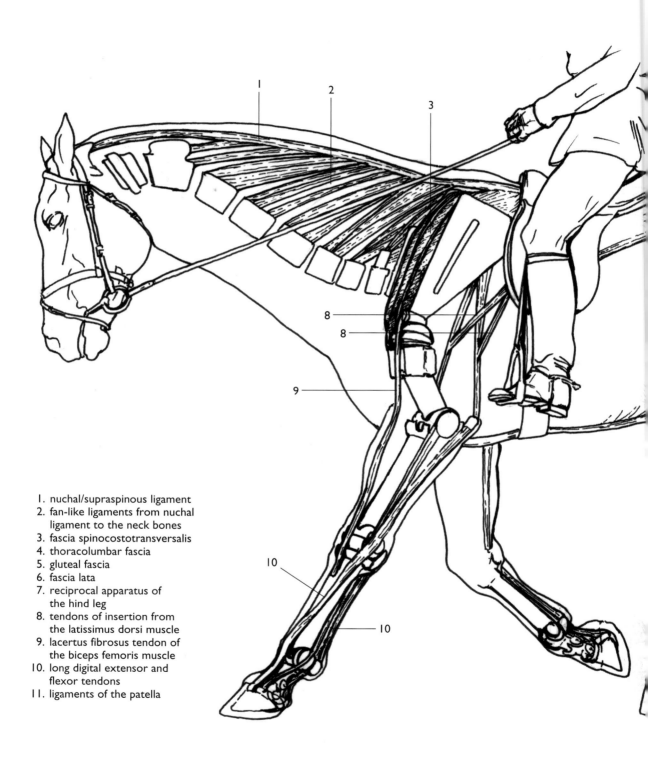

1. nuchal/supraspinous ligament
2. fan-like ligaments from nuchal ligament to the neck bones
3. fascia spinocostotransversalis
4. thoracolumbar fascia
5. gluteal fascia
6. fascia lata
7. reciprocal apparatus of the hind leg
8. tendons of insertion from the latissimus dorsi muscle
9. lacertus fibrosus tendon of the biceps femoris muscle
10. long digital extensor and flexor tendons
11. ligaments of the patella

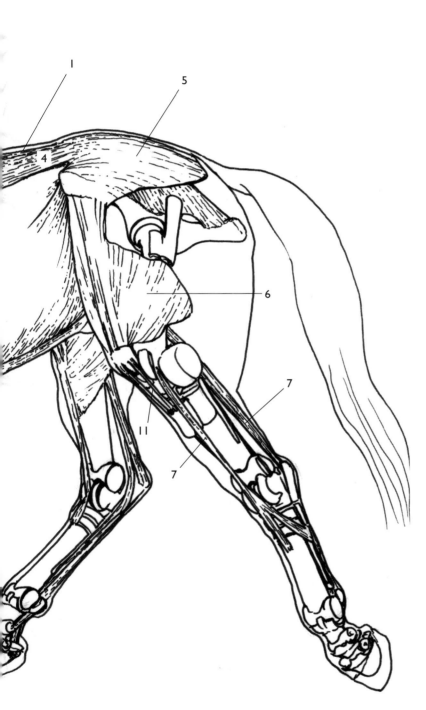

The connective tissue 'harness' takes the muscle power to the bones. Fundamentally, it is by virtue of this harness that we can ride the horse at all. Its presence means that we can apply a small amount of pressure to one point of the horse, and, by changing the proprioception in one area, initiate a chain reaction that embraces the whole animal.

The aids to walk, trot, and canter are a logical consequence of the way in which the connective tissue harness is linked together. For example, if the rider does not use his leg, he cannot generate support for his seat. If he has no seat then the contact through the reins will simply be a trial of strength. The horse runs along the ground at full length: he cannot shorten his frame because there is nothing to tell him to do so. He, not the rider, decides when a change of gait becomes necessary – probably when he finds himself sufficiently out of balance.

Once the rider applies the leg aid and lifts the horse's back underneath him, the resulting traction over the croup via the fascia engages the hindquarters and applies traction to the fascia around the stifle joint. The stifle, hock and hind fetlock mechanisms are coupled so that any increased flexion of the stifle immediately incorporates the whole of the hind leg.

Traction along the back is sustained by traction through the abdominal fascia, and the springiness of the hind limb stride can begin to lift the forehand, making it light in the rider's hand.

This network of communication travels around the body along tracks laid down by fascia, tendons, and ligaments. Muscles provide the power, but connective tissues provide the fluency. In order to move the horse through changes of gait, the rider has to adjust the tension of the 'harness' to the right length, otherwise the horse just flaps along regardless.

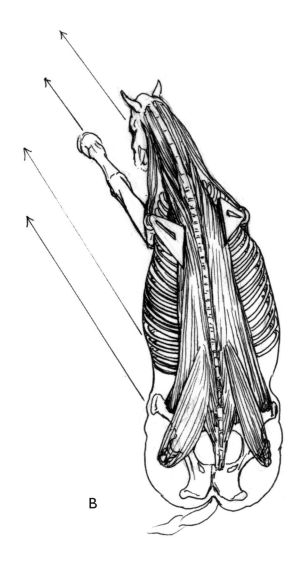

A

B

The rider's legs can be used symmetrically, to promote forwards movement in a straight line, or asymmetrically, to maintain length-bend, or to keep the horse on the correct leg at the canter. The rider's inside leg increases the upward lift of the inside length of the horse, which enables the horse's fore and hind limbs to spring forwards. The rider's outside leg maintains the lift through the outside lumbar muscles and prevents the horse from swinging his quarters outside the framework of the intended figure.

Exactly the same system of support is necessary for lateral work. What changes is the influence of the rider's body weight, which acts through his pelvis to move the horse diagonally. However, the elastic suspension of both sides of the back, along the long back muscles, under the shoulder blades and up through the neck, is just as relevant.

The same considerations apply as at the most basic gaits. The freedom of the inside shoulder and inside base of the neck is vital, whether the horse is looking in the direction of lateral movement, or away from it.

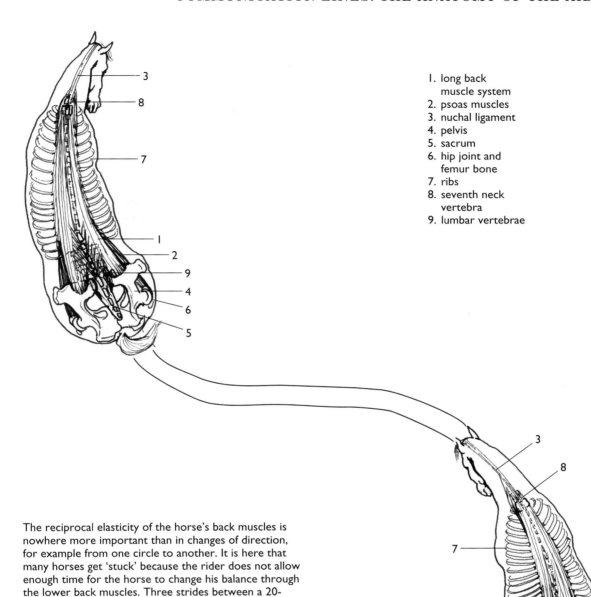

1. long back
   muscle system
2. psoas muscles
3. nuchal ligament
4. pelvis
5. sacrum
6. hip joint and
   femur bone
7. ribs
8. seventh neck
   vertebra
9. lumbar vertebrae

The reciprocal elasticity of the horse's back muscles is nowhere more important than in changes of direction, for example from one circle to another. It is here that many horses get 'stuck' because the rider does not allow enough time for the horse to change his balance through the lower back muscles. Three strides between a 20-metre (66-foot) circle to the left and one to the right is all it takes for the horse to keep himself upright while changing his lateral flexion. It also gives the rider time to change his leg position so that his outside leg now becomes his inside leg and vice versa.

The smooth change of bend, which becomes more demanding for the lumbar muscles as the horse is asked for more collection, also weighs heavily on a small group of muscles underneath the spine: the psoas group. These muscles are the first to initiate the movement of the hind legs. Unless they are supple, the back remains stiff and unyielding, and any semblance of bend is left entirely to the rider's imagination.

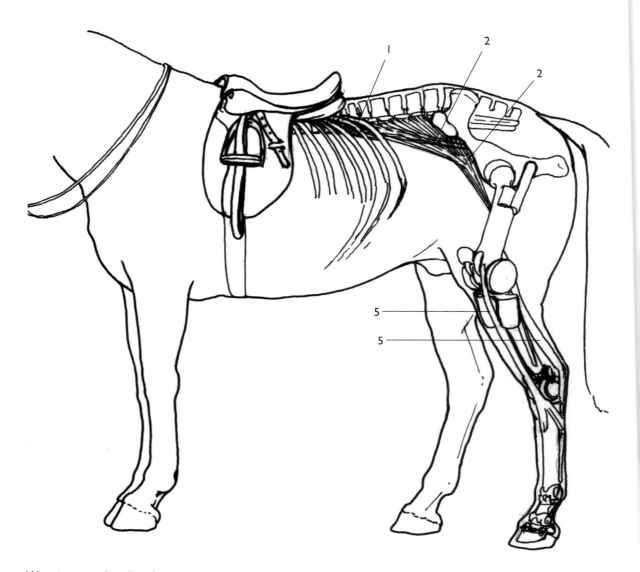

Warming up and cooling down.

The psoas group of muscles, located directly under the horse's lumbar spine, originate from just inside the ribcage and from under the lumbar vertebrae to the inside of the thigh bone. They flex the hip and help to brace the lower back.

The moment we put the saddle on the horse's back, these muscles tighten. It is a natural reaction to the effect of the saddle's weight, or even just its presence. The effect is increased when we mount up. As long as these muscles are tight, we can and should expect no engagement from the hindquarters. They behave like a rigid tow bar under the spine. They have to be released before they, and the rest of the back muscles, can begin to expand and contract fluently.

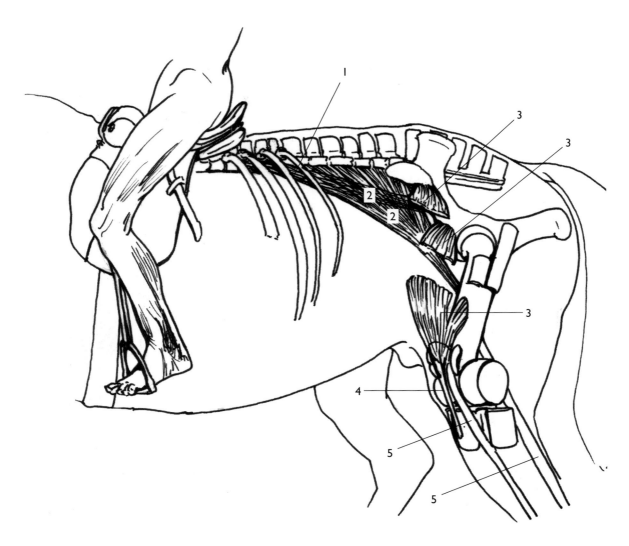

1. psoas minoris
   muscle
2. iliopsoas muscle
   group
3. quadriceps muscles
   (cut away)
4. patella ligament
5. reciprocal apparatus

There is some controversy over the merits of the rising trot and turns on the forehand. But in respect of the psoas muscles, these exercises help to release the lower back, without which the action of both the quadriceps muscles and the reciprocal apparatus is, literally, stifled!

What is certain is that keeping these muscles supple is the purpose of warming up, and cooling down. Too few riders think of these phases as being part of the overall pattern of exercise. Yet, like a gradual crescendo and decrescendo, the work should begin and end with loosening: otherwise the notes might be in place but they won't make any music.

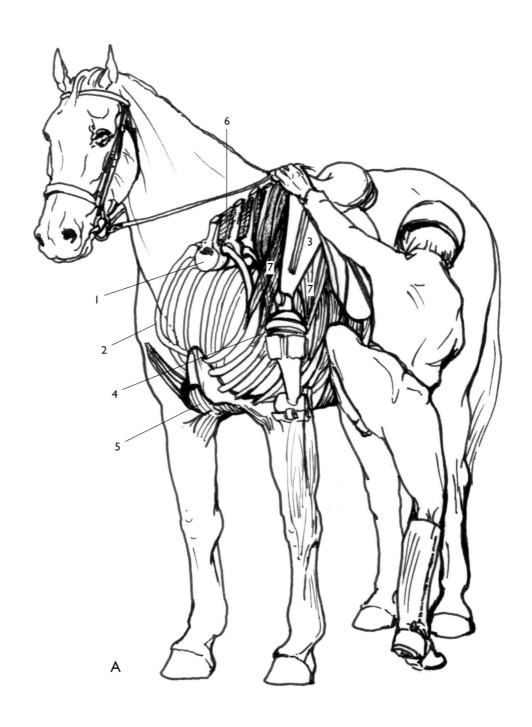

A

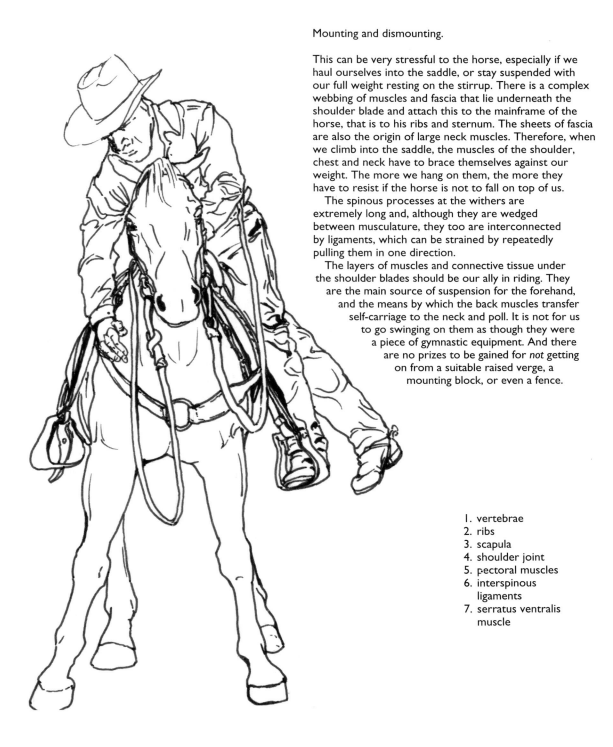

Mounting and dismounting.

This can be very stressful to the horse, especially if we haul ourselves into the saddle, or stay suspended with our full weight resting on the stirrup. There is a complex webbing of muscles and fascia that lie underneath the shoulder blade and attach this to the mainframe of the horse, that is to his ribs and sternum. The sheets of fascia are also the origin of large neck muscles. Therefore, when we climb into the saddle, the muscles of the shoulder, chest and neck have to brace themselves against our weight. The more we hang on them, the more they have to resist if the horse is not to fall on top of us.

The spinous processes at the withers are extremely long and, although they are wedged between musculature, they too are interconnected by ligaments, which can be strained by repeatedly pulling them in one direction.

The layers of muscles and connective tissue under the shoulder blades should be our ally in riding. They are the main source of suspension for the forehand, and the means by which the back muscles transfer self-carriage to the neck and poll. It is not for us to go swinging on them as though they were a piece of gymnastic equipment. And there are no prizes to be gained for *not* getting on from a suitable raised verge, a mounting block, or even a fence.

1. vertebrae
2. ribs
3. scapula
4. shoulder joint
5. pectoral muscles
6. interspinous ligaments
7. serratus ventralis muscle

5 Mixed Messages: the Anatomy of Rider Errors

'Send us three and fourpence. We're going to a dance.' Imagine you're in a busy shopping centre, or at a railway station, and you get this message on your mobile. Apart from finding the reference to the old currency a bit odd, you might think the request a bit of a cheek. But, grammatically, it makes perfect sense, and it's not impossible that someone might ask for money for a night out.

Now imagine you're a telecommunications operator in a war zone, and you've just heard the same message – or think you have. The grammar is just the same, but it now makes no sense at all. What you should have heard was: 'Send us reinforcements. We're going to advance.' Unfortunately, something happened to distort the message during the process of transmission.

In the 1990s, the great Olympic rider Dr Reiner Klimke came to Britain to give a number of dressage clinics. During the course of one teaching session, he told one of the participants to canter on. The rider gave his horse the command, and the horse obediently struck off – on the wrong leg. Dr Klimke's response was: 'Well, if you want the horse to do something, you do have to give him the right aids.'

It was meant as a snub, and, since the rider was a member of the national team, and this was said in front of a large audience, it was probably taken as such. But it was also a cautionary lesson for us all. Because, no matter how accurate we think we're being, when we're riding, it's amazing how many messages make perfect sense when they leave our brains, but become completely distorted by the time they reach our arms and legs.

What seems perfectly reasonable to the human mind, can, for various reasons, seem perfectly unreasonable to the horse. The horse is then expected to convert these messages into some sort of action, even though they might have arrived at his flanks and mouth, by way of a game of anatomical Chinese whispers.

The first problem the horse has to contend with is 'handedness': the handedness of humans, and the supposed handedness (or 'natural bent') of the horse himself. Whether or not the horse really does have a natural bend is not entirely clear. On the one hand, some scientists have tried to attribute this 'bend' to the horse's foetal position in the womb. On the other hand, if this were so, one would expect to see uneven foot wear in wild populations of horses and ponies, which doesn't seem to be the case. Nevertheless, Klimke believed that young horses had a left bias, and that early schooling exercises involved teaching the horse to go straight. Other great riders have made similar assumptions.

However, it cannot be ignored that, from a very early age, the domestic horse is accustomed to having everything done to him almost exclusively from the near side, either because most humans are right-handed or because humans simply follow tradition. If, for example, you are fed, haltered, tacked up, led about, always from the left side, it doesn't take long before you learn to anticipate this direction, and adjust your mental and physical behaviour accordingly. Therefore, the jury is still out as to whether a genuine distinction can be made between the left and right sides of the equine brain. But there certainly is such a distinction in the human brain, and it is one that has an enormous effect on our ability to give aids of the same quality with both the left and right sides of our bodies.

Most of us take our right hand and leg for granted. We assume that we have the same sense of touch and strength in the left hand and leg. Invariably this is not the case. The left hand tends to over-compensate because its skill in manipulation is less well practised. The left leg behaves similarly because we perceive it to be lacking in strength. The result is that the left hand becomes tense and causes the left arm to make an awkward kink at the wrist or elbow. The left hand has difficulty staying level with the right: it advances slightly forward. The left knee is drawn up, and the left leg clenches the horse with the calf, or seeks extra security by clutching the horse's side with the heel.

To the rider, these postural adjustments have no significance. They are a natural consequence of the left–right brain organization; they are part of natural human movement. However, to the horse, every touch, every shift in weight, of the rider's body, equates to an aid. Unfortunately, the mismatch between left and right brings the aids into conflict. Then the horse has to choose between the two sides and will often, understandably, choose the most penetrating.

Right-handedness in riding, however slight, has enormous consequences, not just for general work on the left rein, but for all work that involves bending through left-handed corners or left circles. (Most people spend more of their time schooling their horses to the left than they do to the right.)

The problem with any sort of bend, whether to the left or right, is that the word 'bend' only evokes a mental image of flexion. Yet, to be sustainable, the 'bend' of the horse *must* incorporate 'lift'. The horse has to take shorter steps with the fore and hind legs on the inside of the circle than with those on the outside. Therefore, he must lift himself through the chest and abdomen. Only then can he create enough space under his body to gather his legs underneath him.

To achieve this, the rider must use the supporting function of his inside leg – often referred to as the 'driving' leg. The leg 'drives' because it serves to keep the horse's body level. This enables the horse to load his inside and outside legs in equal measure, rather than incline his body weight to the inside of the track, like a tilting train. Used correctly, the rider's inside leg is a helping leg. But, on left bends, it is more often a hampering leg.

The most common fault in riding any figure involving the left bend is that instead of taking up (shortening) the inside rein to establish the change of direction, the rider stiffens the left arm and wrist, and lowers the left hand. The rider then tries to increase the pressure of the left leg by kinking to the right, usually at the waist. This throws the rider's seat towards the outside of the bend, and takes the pressure off the left seat bone (or it moves it uncomfortably close to the horse's spine). This defeats the whole purpose of the leg aid.

The right hand, instead of maintaining a contact with the outside rein and creating a sequence of matching steps along the outside length of the horse, tries to 'lend a hand'. It reaches forwards, thereby releasing the parallel steps that make the bend. The horse's body becomes a series of two straight lines, one along the neck, and one along the body, which are loosely joined by an angle in front of the shoulder. The rider now has a very uneven perch. He inevitably falls forward with his left shoulder, probably looks down to the ground, and, invariably, holds his breath. (If this sounds very uncomfortable, imagine what it feels like to the horse.)

The consequence of human right-handedness for the horse, is that he learns to list into the left bend. The right side of his body, to all intents and purposes, moves in a straight line. The right hind leg has push, but the left side of the body is blocked by the rider's unconsciously unforgiving left hand and leg. Therefore, the left hind leg has no means of equalling the push of its right counterpart. The horse throws himself across the diagonal at every stride, from right hind to left fore, and has to shorten the stride of the left foreleg to keep his balance.

The force of impulsion from the right hind can be such that the left brachiocephalic and pectoral muscles have to continually brace themselves against the impact. This, again, reduces the forwards stride through the bend – just when the horse needs it most. When these muscles run out of steam, the pressure is borne last, but not least, by the vertebrae at the base of the neck – the area in front of the first rib. Eventually the horse will go lame because the lower part of the limb, with only lateral/medial ligaments to support the joints, cannot sustain this sort of movement indefinitely. However, before the lameness becomes clinically obvious, many horses develop tightness or even considerable soreness in the muscles and connective tissues around the left shoulder joint.

Right-handedness is a fact of human life. Many horses acquire the same one-sidedness because that is how they are ridden. It's not, of course, the end of the world, but it's up to riders to make a conscious effort to develop an awareness of their left sides. And that can take a lot of practice.

If 'handedness' is a source of confusion to the horse, it perhaps does not seem as muddleheaded as 'leglessness'. For example, we're probably all agreed that, in some manner or form, the rider's legs make the horse go forwards. Whether they are used continuously or intermittently, calmly or abruptly, it is the legs that cause the horse to increase his speed, lengthen his stride, or increase his elevation. But what about the downward transitions?

In order to change down the gears, the horse has two possible choices. He can run on, gradually slowing the pace, until he naturally gravitates from canter, to trot, to walk. Or he can change pace instantly, by suspending the forehand and back, and changing the amount of impulsion from the hindquarters.

There's nothing wrong with the first way, except that it takes time. However, if the horse is required to make a transition immediately, on the rider's command, he has to make room underneath his body for his hind legs. It doesn't matter whether be suddenly puts the brakes on with the front legs, or, if he's working in true collection, initiates the braking action from the back: the hind legs have to be in a position to absorb what is the equivalent of a momentary 'reverse thrust'. If, at this critical moment, the rider takes the legs away from the horse's sides, then he lets the bottom fall out of the horse's undercarriage.

The logic of the leg aid is that in any downward transition (including the transition to halt), the rider's legs give the horse's body more support, not less. For this reason, the legs must stay in contact with the horse: to maintain the reflexes through the back muscles, and the muscles of the abdomen and chest. This enables the horse to continue bracing his back under the weight of the rider, rather than the rider periodically dumping all his weight onto the horse's spine. (Horses that hollow their backs at every downward transition have invariably come to expect this experience – and are doing their best to avoid it.)

The timing of the supporting leg in downward transitions is relevant to all styles of riding, not just to European-style dressage. It is particularly relevant to Western-style riding when this is practised on non-Western breeds of horses. The conformation of the American Quarter Horse, for example, is such that the base of the neck, the front of the chest, and the medial attachments of the forelegs are powerfully supported by a thick collar of muscles. In addition to this, these horses are stockily built over the loins and quarters. When the Western rider wants to make a sharp transition, he can do so using his body weight, in combination with the bit if necessary. The rider sits far back off the horse's forehand, because of the construction of the Western saddle, and, as the horse brakes and drops his quarters, he can shift his weight even further back towards the loins. The horse can absorb the impact of the transition through his pectoral muscles, because that is how he's built. In addition to this, the straight leg of the Western horseman (although it is at this moment pointing forwards), stays in contact with the horse's body through the inner thigh. This is probably all it takes to maintain the bracing of the chest and abdomen – in this breed of horse.

However, in horses that are conformationally longer limbed, more high withered, or slender backed, this style of riding needs serious consideration. Like using a family saloon car to compete in a world class rally championship, they are likely to break down because of the strain on the suspension – in other words, the area of connective tissues under the shoulders, which is supported by the pectoral sling. For horses that do not have the structural resilience to cope with the stringent demands of Western-style riding, riders should take a leaf out of the book of classical dressage and apply the tactical use of the leg aid in all downward transitions.

The influence of the aids is something all riders have to grapple with, pupils and masters alike. However, there is a more subtle influence, which is rather harder to fathom than that of uneven hands or missing legs: namely, the fact that horses often become like their humans! Of course, they don't do so – not in the same way that we imagine dogs to look like their owners – but if a person rides with a stiff lower back, you can bet money that the horse will go with a stiff back, too. If a person hunches their shoulders, the horse will hunch his shoulders. If the rider draws his neck down into the chest, the horse will do

the same. Changing the horse is not such a problem. Changing the human is quite another matter.

Does this mean we are doomed before we even get into the saddle? Not a bit of it. If we look at the great rider of the Spanish Riding School, Colonel Alois Podhajsky, there is nothing hunched or introverted about his demeanour. What he expresses as a rider, his horses also express, in their self-carriage and their movement. If we look at the great event riders, they could never take on such enormous fences if their overall posture was not open and positive – and neither could their horses.

The movement therapist, Feldenkrais, said that 'all negative emotion is expressed as flexion'. He was talking about humans. Yet we have to ask ourselves – when we're working our horses in, and making them go in the currently popular 'long and low' position – what emotion we, ourselves, are expressing. Is it not perhaps we, the riders, that are in the long and low position – not just mentally, but physically, too.

Riding is a complex skill. It requires both physical awareness and mental dexterity. The horse naturally has both of these, otherwise he would not have survived as a species. Humans have awareness, too. But humans have a curious obstinacy. For only humans are capable of repeatedly carrying out the same action while repeatedly expecting to get a different result. The horse would never do such a thing: he'd either give up, or try a different tack. Think about it the next time you ask your horse, for the third time, to 'canter left', and, for the third time, he gives you 'canter right'.

There's a lot we can improve about our riding by ensuring our messages always make sense to the horse. The horse undoubtedly has a sense of humour, but the one thing he can't do is smile. Only humans can smile. And, sometimes, that's all it takes to ride well.

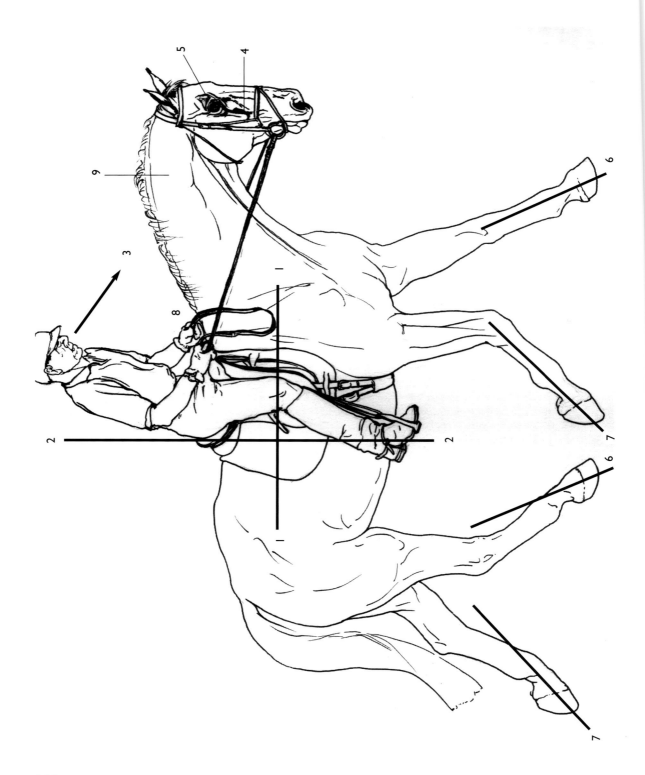

In the strictest sense, the aids consist of small amounts of physical pressure applied to strategic points on the horse's body to stimulate simple reflex actions. Each stimulus has a knock-on effect, so that a chain of messages is set in motion and culminates in the horse adopting a specific posture. This posture should not be unnatural, but it should allow the horse to carry the rider without strain to his muscles, tendons and joints. However, if the aids really did consist of purely physical stimuli, there would be little fascination in trying to perfect the art. It could be done by robots – to better effect! What makes us want to ride – and ride well – is the human element, the fact that every human being has a different sense of the aids (what we now call rider 'feel').

In reality, the aids consist of a hierarchy of stimuli:

• Simple reflexes, caused by intermittent pressure on a muscle/nerve group and its tendons (like our patella reflex, but used continually to regulate the rhythm of the stride).
• Physical manipulation of muscles: the back-up system, when we need to reinforce the aids, or intervene in the action of the horse – for whatever reason.
• 'Extraneous circumstances' (to borrow from General Decarpentry): situations or objects that work to our advantage in helping the horse understand what we require of him. For example, a road junction for traffic sense, or polework for back suppling, These circumstances can be planned or improvised; they can be a source of support – or a cause of distraction.
• Rider emotions. Any form of movement is allied to the emotions, but riding is especially so. The rider's state of mind plays a huge part in how well his own muscles perform. Anger and aggression are usually undesirable emotions because they cause tension. But sentimentality is also dangerous because it makes us indecisive, and limp.

It is the intervention of our psyche that determines what sort of messages we send to the horse, whether they are clear and unmistakable, or muddle-headed and confused. Getting the balance just right can be a matter of the strictest appraisal of our position in the saddle. For example, the horse in this illustration seems to be working 'nicely'. He looks to be reasonably well balanced, with good forward momentum. There are no worry lines around his mouth, and the rider is not using a great deal of effort to keep him moving. But although the pair make a pleasant picture, their efforts are not yet quite satisfactory.

1. There is a horizontal line from the horse's hip joint to a point midway down the scapula. The point of rotation for the forelimb is approximately at the top third of the scapula. This means that the horse has the potential to come off the forehand but, at this moment, has not yet done so.
2. The vertical line that should connect the rider's ankle to his hip, shoulder, and ear, passes through the back of the saddle. The rider is tipping forwards.
3. The rider's gaze is directed downwards, over the horse's shoulder. He is not riding towards any particular point in the arena, nor is he projecting this to his horse.
4 and 5. The horse's head is vertical, but if we look carefully at the ridge of the cheek bone (4) and the small muscle above the eye (5), both are angled slightly behind the vertical. The horse's head is obedient, but his brain is not really engaged.

6. and 7. It should be possible to draw parallel lines through each pair of diagonal legs. The lines numbered 6 are parallel to each other, as are those labelled 7, but they do not coincide with the angle of the legs. The horse is pictured just at the moment of suspension in the trot, but the rhythm of his diagonal strides must be uneven.
8. The rider's hands are not parallel. The left hand is trying to come across the withers, while the right hand is pulling back. The rider is trying to offset the pull by opening the ring finger. Somewhere along the right arm there is tension.
9. The horse's neck is bent over between the second and third neck vertebrae. The highest point of the neck should be just behind the ears at the poll, but it won't be achieved until the rider is sitting comfortably: then the story can begin!

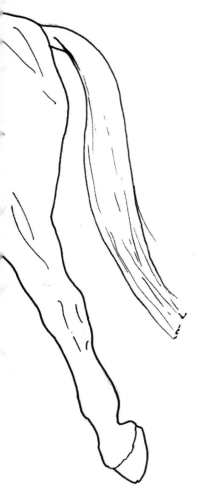

Whereas the horse in the illustration on page 138 has the potential to come up in front, this horse is being 'ground' into the ground. He is being forced to stare at the ground in front of him and the head is being turned to the left in an attempt to get some sort of lateral flexion.

The rider is looking down over the horse's left shoulder. She might be doing so with the best of intentions, but her neck is making the same unfortunate twist that she is creating in the horse. Both she and the horse are inclining the inside (left) shoulder. The only difference is that there is no weight resting on the shoulders of the rider.

The right hand is higher than the left hand and yielding to the pull of the horse's neck muscles as he bends. There Is no continuous line from the left elbow to the horse's mouth. The left hand desperately wants to achieve something, but it is not fully under control, so it has resorted to pulling. To soften the effect, the ring finger has opened.

In this horse, everything is literally riding on the left brachiocephalic muscle. This muscle is locked, and it's locked short. That means all other muscles, converging on the neck from the back, are locked long. Although the rider's legs are in a position to lift the horse underneath her, she is having to angle the spur into the horse's side to keep him going.

The rider presumably wants her horse to go forwards, but her messages are muddled. The effect she's creating is downward.

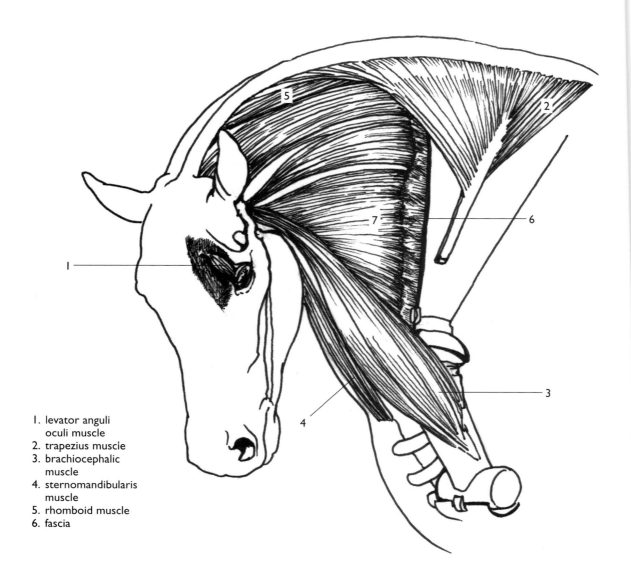

1. levator anguli
   oculi muscle
2. trapezius muscle
3. brachiocephalic
   muscle
4. sternomandibularis
   muscle
5. rhomboid muscle
6. fascia

The upper eyelid of the horse is raised by a small muscle (the levator anguli oculi), which attaches the upper eyelid to the fascia of the forehead. When the horse is working in what often passes for the 'long and low' position, his extremely submissive head carriage forces him to look at the ground in front of his feet. In fact, this is the ground he's just about to leave behind, not the ground he wants to cover. This seems particularly contradictory when what we're trying to achieve is impulsion.

Imagine trying to run forwards with a light, springy step, while at the same time looking at the ground in front of your toes. Your automatic reaction is to raise your head. And if you are prevented from doing so, you raise your eyebrows, tense your neck muscles, and find it extremely hard to keep your balance. The same is true of the horse. It is possible to see this tension in so small a muscle as the levator anuli oculi! It belies the underlying tension in the neck muscles, which are inevitably locked short.

By contrast, the horse moving at liberty has no difficulty in seeing where he's going. However, he is not having to carry any weight on his back: his self-carriage does not have to accommodate the presence of a rider.

The correct head carriage of the horse, when he is ridden, must do two things:

• It must correctly tense the nuchal/supraspinous ligament, which extends from the poll to the hindquarters, and on which many of the neck and back muscles, and fascia, insert.
• It must allow the horse to see where he's going.

When the horse is working in collection, the head will be just in front of the vertical. From this position, the horse can cover the ground – without looking at it.

Disengaging the hindquarters.

This is a method of control advocated by Pat Parelli in his Natural Horse-Man-Ship method. The rider brings (in this case) the right hand to his mid-section, and lifts the rein (A). The horse is trained to give his head 'freely', which uncouples the neck from the rest of the horse's body, and takes the hindquarters out of action. The concept behind this action is one of instantaneously slackening all the connective tissue in the neck and shoulders: the nuchal ligament, the fan-like ligament attachments to the neck bones, and the fascial attachments of the neck muscles under the shoulders. The horse is prevented from bracing the neck muscles, planting the forehand, and pushing off in any direction with the hind legs.

However, the suddenness of this intervention is drastic. It's like a lorry jackknifing. It causes the hindquarters to momentarily swing sideways, locking the patella reflex and disabling the

144

1. line of the neck vertebrae visualized through the head
2. long back muscles
3. latissimus dorsi muscle feeding into teres major muscle on medial side of the shoulder
4. gluteus medius muscle
5 and 6. tensor fascia lata, and quadriceps muscles
7. patella ligaments
8. reciprocal apparatus
9. tendons of the supraspinatus muscle

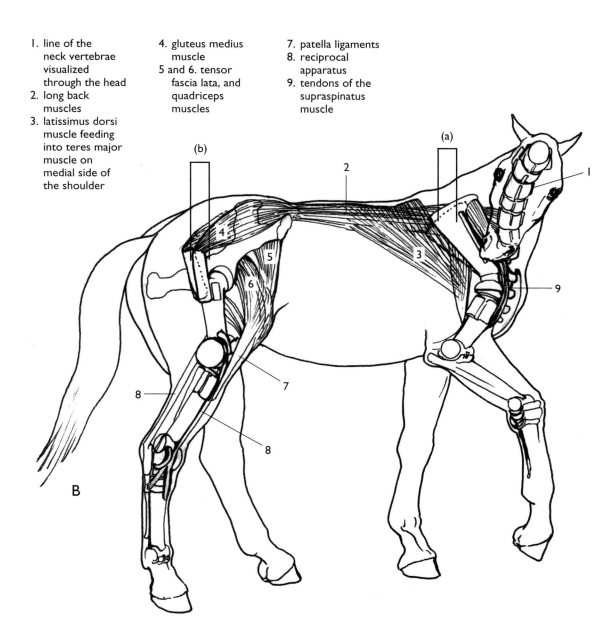

reciprocal apparatus at one hit. Much of the energy is absorbed by the ligaments at the sides of the joints (collateral ligaments). The rest, which has nowhere to go, must be dissipated through the back and the shoulders.

The effect of this ambush on the horse's movement, combined with a severe twist of the neck, puts tremendous strain on the muscles at the base of the neck and on the connective tissues that hold the neck bones in the area of the first rib. It causes a sudden shift in the position of key skeletal levers, such as: (a) the scapula (shoulder blade); (b) the trochanter major of the femur (thigh bone). The energy of movement has to be absorbed though the muscles, or dissipated through the joints of the stifle, shoulder, and neck vertebrae (B).

They say dogs and their owners often show an uncanny likeness, but what about horses and their riders? For example, imagine this horse when he is trotting round his paddock. Would he do so with a tilted head carriage, a fixed neck, and tight thigh muscles? Probably not.

Yet, under saddle, he reflects, in virtually every detail, the posture of his rider. She is bracing her neck, and looking downwards. There is tension in her arms, which are not flexed comfortably at the elbow, and she is seeking the horse's side, with the spurs, by drawing the lower leg upwards and tightening the knee.

Because the continuous line from the horse's mouth to the rider's elbow is interrupted by a kink at the wrist, the rider is unconsciously yielding to the pressure by opening the ring finger.

The horse is attentive, and the rider is caring. But the horse's back is not lifted, so the rider is perched, not seated. Without a seat, she cannot be carried, and neither can her hands. They are looking for support.

If this rider's aids were in the form of radio waves, they would be confused by static interference. And that is just what we've got here: a static horse.

In this picture, the horse is obviously forward going. But would he go forwards, in this posture, if he was at liberty?

The rider is turning into a bend. As she does so, she looks down over the horse's shoulder. The kink in the left wrist, and the extension of the ring finger, are indicators of tension in the left arm. The contact is not elastic; the rider is about to pull the horse into the circle. The fingers of the right hand are closed, but this hand is creeping forwards, to open the way for the horse to drift out through the shoulder. Not only is the rider looking down but she is pulling her head down towards her chest. The muscles in front of her throat are tight, and in all probability her trapezius muscles (over the shoulder blades) will be braced (otherwise she would tip too far forwards). The horse's ventral neck muscles are exactly like those of the rider's: his neck is overbent.

The muscles on the underside of the neck are locked short, blocking the lift of the forehand through the base of the neck, The activity of the hind limbs wants to create forward motion along the back, but there is nowhere for it go. It has to be absorbed through the pectoral muscles at the front of the chest.

The message, when it left the rider's brain, was undoubtedly, 'Give me lateral flexion, we're going through a bend.' But by the time it reaches the horse, it has become more like, 'Give me that direction, we're going to extend.'

This horse could end up becoming frustrated, notwithstanding the sympathetic look on his rider's face.

The stocky cob in this picture shows no length of neck. But then, neither does his rider. The rider's stirrups are just that bit too long, so she is having to reach for them by standing on her toes.

She is not quite out of balance, but neither is she quite in balance. If she were standing on the floor, she could stay upright only by 'jigging' up and down on the spot – which is exactly the effect she's having on her horse.

She is pulling the right hand towards the thigh. But without the support of the right leg against the horse's side, the effect on the mouth is simply one of resistance. The fingers of the right hand are uncomfortable with the contact, so they are spread. The right shoulder is turned forwards and inwards in an attempt to enforce the aid. The horse's shoulder imitates that of the rider, exactly.

The wonderful hindquarters of this horse, which could be engaged to lift him off the forehand, are trailing. His 'bum' looks big in this picture, and it's just possible his rider is self-conscious about hers, too.

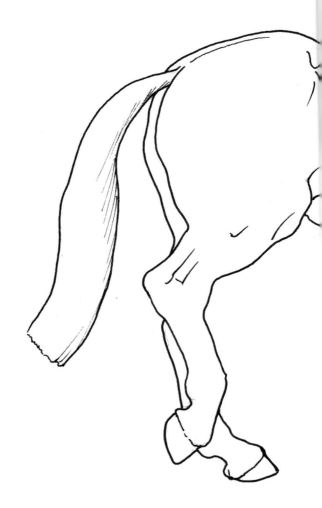

Whilst only the very few can carry their horses
successfully and safely through Olympian exertions
such as these, it is well within everybody's capability...

...to protect their horse's anatomy by beginning and ending each and every training session with an active walk on a loose rein.

Whatever problems we encounter during schooling, however many knotty and convoluted messages were of our own making, we can unravel them all, in an instant, by allowing the horse to stretch through the base of his neck.

He must walk forwards in self-carriage, and he might just breathe a little sigh of relief. But as long as we adhere strictly to this principle, as long as we allow the brachiocephalic muscles room to unwind after exertion, there will be no lasting ill-effects – even on a bad day.

There's no tension in a smile, and every ride should end with one.

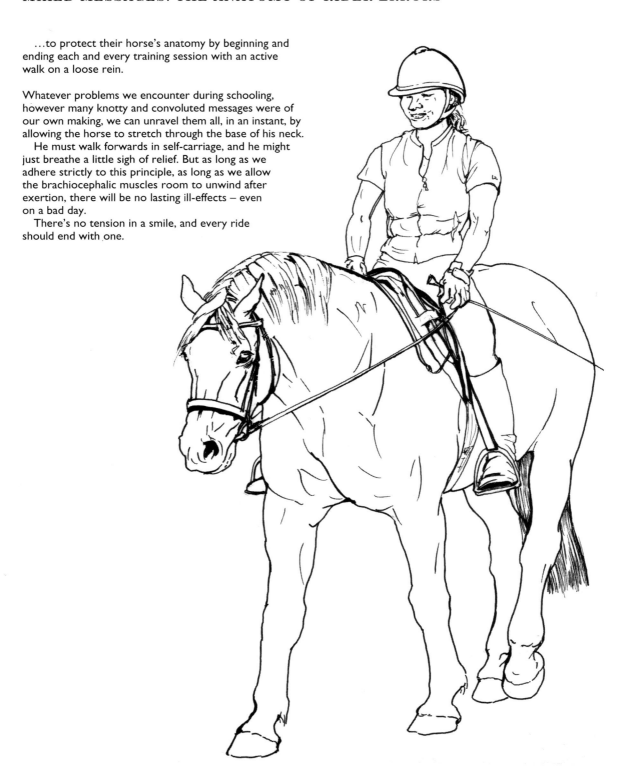

Postscript ─────────────────────────

Of course, all the reading in the world is no substitute for 'doing'. You can describe, in words and pictures, the most sumptuous meal to a hungry man, but it is unlikely to satisfy his appetite for the real thing. In the end, theory cannot replace practical experience.

Once, at a showjumping yard, I was asked what I thought of a Grade A mare. Her conformation was strikingly awful – she was sickle-hocked, roach-backed, and over at the knee, which is what I said. 'What does that matter', was the reply. 'She puts herself together, when she's jumping.'

There are many examples of horses who have become champions in spite of, or perhaps because of, their faulty conformation. Equally, there are many horsemen who can look a horse in the eye and discover, there, the source of his ability.

At the end of the day, the art of riding is as much about self-belief as it is about muscles and bones. For, in the words of the philosopher Krishnamurti in *The Impossible Question*:

> When you see 'what is', it does not demand an explanation.

Select Bibliography ──

In the course of preparing this book, it has been necessary to consult varoius sources of riding wisdom. There are many good books and articles available to the rider, and everybody surely has his or her favourite. Of course, everyone should know their Xenophon, or their 'Newcastle'. The vision of these horsemen is enduring. But, if the author were to be banished to a desert island – one that had an arena and some horses, of course – she would ask to take the following books. With these under the palm tree, it would never be necessary to look out for passing ships...

Exploring Dressage Technique: Journeys into the Art of Classical Riding
Paul Belasik
(J.A. Allen 1994)

This book appears to start with the finer details of *passage* and *piaffe*, and work upwards from there. However, it is, in fact, a detailed study of pace and rhythm, and the way in which the rider can affect these – at any level. It's extremely readable – even for us ordinary mortals.

Academic Equitation
General Decarpentry
(First published 1949)
(Trans. Nicole Bartle, J.A. Allen, 1971)

Of all the texts available, this is my personal favourite. Decarpentry stands out for his humility and sensitivity, as well as for his incredible understanding of the horse's anatomy at work. Anyone who is in any doubt about which bit to use should consult the chapter entitled 'The Mouthpiece'.

François Baucher: The Man and His Method
Hilda Nelson
(J.A. Allen 1992)

This book includes translations of *Dialogues on Equitation* (1835) and *New Methods of Horsemanship* (1842). Baucher's exercises for suppling the jaw, poll, and neck are not practised in this way today. But they are extraordinarily effective. His understanding of the compromises that have to be made in order to ride horses with awkward conformation is a source of inspiration, as is his 'dialogue' between the God of the Quadrupeds, a Horse, and a Horseman.

Dialogues on Equitation
François Baucher
See *François Baucher: The Man and His Method.*

New Method of Horsemanship
François Baucher
See *François Baucher: The Man and His Method.*

Dressage in Lightness
Sylvia Loch
(J.A. Allen, 2000)

This is a detailed description of how to ride all the different paces and figures in dressage. It is